the Hunger for
ECSTASY

the Hunger for
ECSTASY

FULFILLING THE SOUL'S
NEED FOR PASSION
AND INTIMACY

Jalaja Bonheim, Ph.D.

An Imprint of Rodale Books

Jacket and Interior Design: Lynn N. Gano
Jacket Photograph: Chromatone Images/Index Stock Imagery

Library of Congress Cataloging-in-Publication Data

Bonheim, Jalaja.
    The hunger for ecstasy : fulfilling the soul's need for passion and intimacy / Jalaja Bonheim.
        p.   cm.
    Includes bibliographical references.
    ISBN 1–57954–116–X   hardcover
    1. Ecstasy.   2. Spiritual life.   I. Title.
    BL626 .B66   2001
    291.4—dc21   00-010931

Distributed to the book trade by St. Martin's Press

2   4   6   8   10   9   7   5   3   1   hardcover

Visit us on the Web at www.rodalebooks.com, or call us toll-free at (800) 848-4735.

─── OUR PURPOSE ───

*We publish books that empower
people's minds and spirits.*

Contents

INTRODUCTION

Ecstasy is what everyone craves—not love or sex, but a hot-blooded, soaring intensity, in which being alive is a joy and thrill. That enravishment doesn't give meaning to life, and yet without it life seems meaningless.

—Diane Ackerman

If you think of ecstasy as an exceptional state enjoyed now and then by exceptional people, I hope this book will inspire you to think again. Ecstasy is neither a luxury nor an aberration. It is our birthright.

We all need ecstasy in our lives. That state of rapture, of bliss, of feeling totally in love with life is an essential nutrient without which we cannot thrive. Yet if ecstasy is spiritual food, we are a nation of starving people. Children of a culture that ignores the hunger for ecstasy, we know no other way of life and therefore assume that our ecstasy-deprived state is normal. In fact, it is terribly unhealthy and has a disastrous effect on our communities.

"What does it all mean?" a deeply depressed client recently asked me. "I don't know," I told her. "I don't think life has a meaning that can fit into words." Yet when we allow ourselves to experience the ecstasy that blossoms in a life lived fully, passionately, and with integrity, life *feels* profoundly meaningful. When life seems barren and meaningless, take notice. Your soul is telling you that it has gone hungry for too long.

All around us we see the symptoms of our disconnection from Spirit and of our unacknowledged hunger for ecstasy—anorexia and bulimia, depression, violence, drug addiction, and broken marriages. Too many people push aside their unspoken yearnings, never articulating their hunger for ecstasy. Ultimately, they give up hope of ever satisfying it. Is it any wonder that we are such consumers of painkillers and antidepressants? Is it any wonder that we are the most overweight people in the world? If we want to create a healthy, peaceful society, we must face the fact that we need joy, rapture, and ecstasy in our lives as much as we need physical food.

> *Ecstasy blows our minds open to a reality that is wild, beautiful, loving, abundant beyond our wildest dreams.*

Ecstasy is a grand word, perhaps too grandiose for your taste—too dramatic, too intense, too outrageous. Ecstasy *is* intense and outrageous. It blows our minds open to a reality that is wild, beautiful, loving, abundant beyond our wildest dreams.

Of course, not everyone is eager to have his or her mind blown wide open. Most of us live quite comfortably within the familiar, if somewhat cramped, confines of our normal mind-set. Like orgasm, ecstasy is a peak experience, and most people don't want to live in constant ecstasy any more than they want to have never-ending orgasms. On the other hand, those who have never experienced orgasm at all sense that they are missing out on one of life's sweetest gifts. You don't need to reach orgasm every time you make love, but if you don't know what orgasm feels like, you haven't connected with the essence of sex. Just as orgasm is the essence of sex, so ecstasy is the essence of life.

We inherited the word *ecstasy* from the ancient Greeks. To them, ecstasy was far more than just a state of heightened pleasure; it was a sacred portal into the realm of the gods. As they saw it, ordinary consciousness could not sustain itself when the majesty, beauty, and sheer force of the Divine struck the fragile human ego like lightening. To survive such an encounter, one had to step out of one's ordinary, small sense of self into a vast, cosmic awareness. They called this process of temporary ego-death *ek-stasis*, which literally means "to cause to stand outside." Ecstasy, they believed, signaled one's entry into the spiritual dimension.

The Greeks were well aware that ecstasy has its price. In the presence of the Divine, the ego-self must die, temporarily if not permanently. We 21st-century Americans, who worship at the altar of the ego and love feeling in control, do not surrender easily to the higher forces. We hunger for spiritual communion but also flee it.

Sanskrit, the language of ancient India, conveys an understanding of ecstasy that complements and expands the Greek. Where the Greek language reflects the curiosity of a youthfully brilliant, intellectually vigorous people, Sanskrit expresses the oceanic consciousness of a very old and holy culture. In Sanskrit, ecstasy is known as *ananda. Ananda* is a state of consciousness, but it is also one of the names of God. To enter into ecstasy is to enter into the mind of God.

"God is the source of ecstasy," the Hindu scriptures declare. "Who could live and breathe, were not the universe permeated by God's ecstasy?"

The Hindu scripture known as the Taittiriya Upanishad reads, "God is joy. From joy all beings are born, by joy they are sustained, and unto joy they shall return." Where joy is present, God is present. In this view, ecstasy involves not so much a leave-taking as a *home-coming*. The sacred realm is our true home, and ecstasy is the joy we feel upon returning home.

In many Hindu scriptures, God is called simply the Self. Similarly, we shall refer to the Divine within each individual as the true Self, as opposed to the ego-based self that believes in the illusion of separation and has yet to realize its true nature. No matter who you are or how you feel, the source of ecstasy lies within you because ecstasy is the experience of your true Self. Your hunger for ecstasy is sacred because it is the hunger for God, which is also the hunger to know and fully become your Self.

Mystics from around the world call us to awaken to the joy that they have discovered at the core of being. Here is Tukaram, a 17th-century Indian ecstatic, trying to tell us where he has been.

> *In the pool of bliss,*
> *Bliss is all ripples.*
> *Bliss is the body*
> *Of bliss.*
> *How can I describe it?*
> *It's too embarrassing.*
> *There's no will left.*[1]

You too can dive into the pool of bliss of which Tukaram speaks. It is available to anyone because at its core, reality is ecstatic. Ecstasy is not something we create but something we make room for. Clear the obstructions and ecstasy will shine forth. Although suffering is an inevitable ingredient of life, it is contained in a greater field of joy.

There are many varieties of ecstasy, just as there are many varieties of love. When the Hindu scriptures say that God is ecstasy, they aren't talking about the kind of ecstasy that people feel when they hear that they just won the lottery. If good fortune makes us ecstatic, bad fortune will make us miserable. This kind of ecstasy is relative; it contains the seeds of suffering, just as day contains the seeds of night and life contains the seeds of death. Conditional ecstasy is a blessing, but it is only a faint echo of the boundless joy of which the Hindu scriptures speak.

Just as there is a love that transcends both love and hate, and a peace that transcends both peace and war—the "peace that passeth all understanding"—so there is an ecstasy that transcends loss and gain. This greater ecstasy does not depend on things going our way, but on our going God's way.

When I speak of Spirit or of God, I'm not referring to something distant or disembodied. Spirit is the very essence of life—vibrant, sensuous, and delighted to be alive. Moreover, spirituality is a very practical matter. A person may go to church or temple or synagogue every day, but if her religious practice has no effect on her daily life, she is not leading a spiritual life. True spirituality has a tangible impact on the world. It transforms the way we get up in the morning, the way we pay our bills, and the way we speak to our neighbors. The kind of spiritual communion this book explores does not split us into two parts—body and spirit—but rather includes the body as an organ of spiritual expression.

Patriarchal religions, including the Judeo-Christian tradition, have, unfortunately, split the physical, everyday world from the spiritual world. They have set up a false dichotomy, severing matter and spirit, body and soul. When you separate things that are meant to be united, such as the physical and the spiritual realms, both suffer. Our everyday lives have suffered because they are no longer suffused with awareness of the sacred. Simultaneously, our spirituality has been drained of its juice and its sensuality. What is left is a specter too thin and too pale to feed the hungry soul.

On the one hand, there is a growing interest in bringing spirituality back into the body and into everyday life. Meditative forms of physical exercise such as yoga and tai chi have entered the mainstream. People are discussing how to approach work as a spiritual practice, how to have an enlightened relationship with money, and how to bring a sense of sacredness into their sexuality, into their relationships, and ultimately into every aspect of their lives.

On the other hand, surprisingly little has been written about the fact that our forms of spiritual practice are in crisis because they have become less and less sensuous over the past few centuries. Eros, once a regular guest wherever people gathered to worship, has, with few exceptions, been banished from our churches, temples, and mosques. Eros is joy, life, and vitality; without the erotic juice, our spirituality dries out and shrivels. As much as this book invites you to open your bedroom to the ecstasy of spiritual communion, it is equally concerned with the question of how we might reclaim the sensuous side of our spiritual practice.

My own journey as an ecstatic began when I went to India to study Indian temple dance, an experience I wrote of extensively in my previous book *Aphrodite's Daughters*. Indian temple dance, an ancient spiritual practice that has been traced back more than a thousand years, combines prayer, worship, and storytelling. The stories the dancer tells are the sacred myths of Hindu mythology.

Indian temple dance belongs to the Tantric branch of Hinduism. According to the Tantric creation myth, the root cause of creation is desire—more specifically, God's desire to make love. The universe came into being because the ecstasy that was God's very essence wanted to be shared. Yet as the primordial Being looked around for a lover, It realized It was all alone. And so the One split Itself into two. One half became the universe, and is called matter, energy, or the goddess Shakti. The other half remained formless and transcendent, and is worshipped as the god Shiva. These two embraced with great joy. Out of their ecstatic love-play, the world was born and is sustained, moment by moment.

Like all creation myths, this is more than a story about the beginning of the world. It reveals how the people of ancient India related to the creative energy of the cosmos and to their own creative energy. It is the myth of a people who held sacred their desire and their sexuality. Believing

We are all participants in the eternal cosmic love affair between the physical and the invisible dimensions.

themselves to be made in the image of the Divine, they found ecstasy in the act of creation and in the giving and receiving of love.

Shiva and Shakti, god and goddess, are not separate from us. Their myths describe the dance of the creative male and female forces within each of us. We are all parts of the Divine, participants in the eternal cosmic love affair between the physical and the invisible dimensions, between god and goddess, matter and spirit. Everything we see, feel, touch, smell, and taste is Spirit incarnate. In fact, our main purpose in life is to make love with the world and with the Spirit that illuminates it from within.

As you might expect, a tradition based on such a myth held love, desire, and sexuality in high esteem. Like Catholic nuns, temple priestesses in ancient India refrained from marrying because they considered themselves "married to God." Unlike Catholic nuns, however, the ancient priestesses did not renounce sex. Not only did they take lovers, they were renowned for their proficiency in the erotic arts. One of the most important roles of a temple priestess was to embody the goddess and, in union with God, to re-enact creation, thereby refreshing and rejuvenating the world. This she might do in either of two ways. First, she might take a human lover, who would become the god to her, while he would worship her as the goddess. Second, she might experience union with God in her meditations and especially in her dancing, which was held to be an ecstatic ritual of erotic communion between herself and her divine lover. Ultimately, all their skills—including meditation, ritual, storytelling, dancing, and the erotic arts—were merely instrumental to their primary calling, which was to make love with God.

Immortalized by masterful sculptors, the stone likenesses of these ancient priestesses still grace the walls of ancient Hindu temples. Some appear alone, others stand wrapped in their lovers' embrace. Many are nude, dressed only in jewels, in their radiant smiles, and in their sinuous, seductive beauty. Their tradition introduced me to the idea that human beings can actually make love with Spirit, and that this kind of lovemaking can yield the most intense ecstasy life has to offer. As my fascination with these mysterious ancestor figures grew, I yearned to feel the same ecstasy that radiated through their bodies and faces. I too wanted to make love with Spirit, with life, with reality.

Yet I had no idea how to go about this. Now and then I touched upon ecstatic states in my dancing, but that wasn't enough—I wanted more. Unfortunately, there are no manuals or guidebooks that teach you how to make love with God. So the question "How do I make love with Spirit?" became my constant companion. In this book, I share with you some of the discoveries I made over the years as I explored the question of what making love with life might mean. I invite you, too, to cultivate a love affair with Spirit. Like any love, this one requires time and attention, but the rewards are great. Spirit is an infinitely creative, potent, generous, patient, and humorous lover.

Each chapter of this book will address an important facet of how we can cultivate intimacy with life. If we are to live our lives as a great love affair, we'll need to learn how to relate wisely to the power of desire. Without desire, we cannot make love—but our desires often get us into trouble. We'll consider how we can become shameless, so that the demon of shame no longer undermines our lovemaking, whether sexual or spiritual. We'll delve into our longing for paradise, and we'll examine the shadow side of ecstasy—the suffering that our hunger for ecstasy can cause, and the painful addictions we sometimes develop in our attempts to satisfy that hunger.

Making love with life is a spiritual practice. Beginning with chapter 6, we'll explore the relationship between discipline and ecstasy, and look at some of the disciplines that can support our journey, especially the practice of presence. From presence is born beauty, which is nothing less than love made manifest—love reflected back to our hungry eyes and hearts.

The spiritual path is not one we are meant to walk alone. We'll talk about ecstatic sexuality—what it is and how to practice it—about the ways our spiritual commitment can enrich and transform our human marriages, and, finally, about the importance of having a community with which to share our journey.

One of my clients refers to himself as a recovering Catholic. His memories of growing up Catholic are of being shamed, guilt-tripped, and disempowered. He emerged from his childhood believing that suffering was good and virtuous and that his hunger for ecstasy was selfish and bad. This may not have been the lesson his teachers intended to teach him, but he learned it nonetheless.

I believe that, like my Catholic client, we are all on a journey of recovery. No matter what religious tradition we come from, we have all been affected by the anti-ecstatic stance of Western civilization and have absorbed its mistrust of nature, of the body, and of pleasure. We have tried to ignore our hunger for ecstasy, and we have tried to placate it with everything money can buy—to no avail. The soul knows what it wants, and it won't settle for less. It knows it came to this world in service and in search of joy.

Every infant is born with a visceral, instinctual knowledge of his connection to Spirit and hence to life. This knowledge need never emerge into conscious awareness. It need never be articulated or conceptualized. Nonetheless, this thread of connection is the foundation of our happiness. If it should weaken or break, we will fall into depression and despair. On the other hand, if we trace the thread of our happiness back to its source, and if we succeed in making intimate, direct, personal contact with Spirit, then we will know the true meaning of ecstasy.

Some people are content knowing Spirit from a distance, like a child who is happy knowing that her mother is around somewhere in the house. Others live only for the joy of ecstatic communion. The 19th-century Indian mystic Ramakrishna, for example, moved in and out of ecstasy on an hourly basis. No matter how great or small our appetite for ecstatic experience is, it is essential that we not lose sight of the fragile thread that connects our daily lives to that ineffable reality we call God or Spirit. It is essential that we understand where the source of our happiness lies. Spirituality should not glorify suffering and self-deprivation but reveal a path to ever-greater joy.

"Joy," says the spiritual teacher Emmanuel, "is the God within you standing up, shaking himself off, and beginning to smile."[2] Consider this book, then, a letter of welcome to the God within you.

CHAPTER ONE

Meeting God the Lover

 Who is it that we spend our entire life loving?
—**Kabir**

When, on your deathbed, you look back over your life, what will matter most to you? According to the meditation teacher Jack Kornfield, the question people most often ask themselves at the end of their lives is, "How well have I loved?"[1] Loving well doesn't just mean loving individual people or things. It means loving life itself.

Of course, life isn't always easy to love. It is hard to love life when you just got fired or when you're in the midst of a bitter divorce. The kind of love that lets us embrace any situation, no matter how difficult or upsetting, cannot be sentimental or mushy. This kind of love needs a backbone of fierce commitment. "How well have I loved?" ultimately means "How fully did I engage with life? Did I wholeheartedly grapple with the challenges I faced? Was I honest with myself and others? Did I give life all I had, without holding back? Did I bring to my life the passion of a great lover?" As the Vietnamese Buddhist teacher Thich Nhat Hanh emphasizes, the experience of love does not depend on favorable circumstances; it is available to everyone at all times. "The Buddha's teachings on love are clear. It is possible to live twenty-four hours a day in a state of love. Every movement, every glance, every thought, and every word can be infused with love."[2]

The question of how well we love is important because love holds the key to ecstasy and brings us nearer to God. Love softens us, melts us, and undoes the rigid boundaries that ordinarily separate us. Love is both healing and ecstatic because it reveals to us our unity with others and with the world. Whenever you love something or someone passionately, with all your heart and soul, ecstasy is near. Whatever you love—playing the trombone, writing haiku, playing with your baby, gardening, walking on the beach, tango dancing, skydiving—is your gateway to ecstasy.

Loving God and loving life are inseparable. The world is God's body, and the Spirit that animates it is the breath of God. You might not consider yourself a lover of God, but if you embrace life, you are. On the other hand, someone who considers himself a lover of God but does not embrace life is deluded. That person is in love with an abstraction, not with reality.

Love between human beings takes many forms: love between parent and child, sexual love, brotherly love, love between friends, love between teacher and student, and so on. Every type of relationship we can have with another person provides a model of how we can relate to Spirit, and each type of relationship yields special gifts. For example, if you want to feel safe and protected, meditate on God the mother. If you want wisdom, meditate on God the teacher. But if you are hungry for ecstasy, invite God the lover into your life. Ecstasy is the essence of the relationship between lovers and it is the fruit of communion with God the lover.

Love Songs

It's not hard to see that our society is ravenous for love. Turn on the radio and you'll hear love songs playing on nearly every station. Popular culture gives the impression that life revolves around sex and romance. In reality, the energy and attention people devote to falling in love and making love are minimal compared to the time they spend working, eating, exercising, shopping, managing their money, or watching television. According to polls, many people would rather

Love holds the key to ecstasy. It reveals our unity with others and with the world.

go shopping than make love. But as they amble through the shopping mall, what's blasting over the loudspeakers? Love songs.

Our society is obsessed with sex and romance not because we are oversexed or hopelessly romantic, but because we are ravenous for ecstasy and have been taught for centuries to think of sex and romance as its primary source. We all absorb the myth of romantic love, first through childhood fairy tales, later through movies, novels, and music. Ultimately, the love songs on the radio are not really songs about love at all, but about ecstasy—our longing for it, our brief moments of actually finding it, and our grief upon losing it.

Romance certainly can be an avenue to ecstasy. So can sex. The problem is that these are unreliable access roads. Sometimes we just aren't interested in sex or romance, or perhaps we don't have the ideal sexual partner. Most romances don't turn out to be quite as ecstatic as we hoped. If we depend on romance or sex alone for ecstasy, we're likely to end up feeling frustrated and deprived.

Nonetheless, our intuition does not lie when it insists that ecstasy has something to do with falling in love, with feeling aroused and passionate. Where we go wrong is in assuming that ecstatic love must be the traditional prince-and-princess kind. Ultimately, only one love affair is truly worthy of every love song ever written: our love affair with life. This is the only love that never grows stale but can become more ecstatic with every passing day. Best of all, it is available to all of us, no matter our age or circumstances. This love affair with life (or Spirit or God) is the source of all our other loves. When we nurture and cultivate it, all our relationships will thrive.

The Imagery of Sexual Love

When we speak of God as a lover, we risk offending several groups of people. First, there are the fundamentalists who insist that God must be a father, and *only* a father. Then there are those who might accept the concept of God as mother, but who feel uncomfortable with the sexual implications of God as lover. Raised to believe that God is beyond physical needs and human emotions, or that sex is "dirty," they cringe at the idea of introducing a sexual component into their spirituality. And finally, there are those who don't like to use the word *God* at all because it reminds them of a person—generally a man with a long white beard.

God is not a person and, presumably, it makes no difference to God what metaphors we use in our spiritual practice. It makes a huge difference to us, however. The spiritual journey is an immensely creative, artistic endeavor. Just as a painter chooses a deep cobalt blue or a luscious cinnamon brown in response to some mysterious inner prompting, we each must discover the sacred images that touch our hearts and inspire us. In finding these images, we are not attempting to limit God, but rather we are engaging in sacred play. The images we feel drawn to are invariably those that complement us and help us to become whole.

The most important benefit we gain from cultivating a personal relationship with the Divine is intimacy. As human beings, we are hardwired to need intimate connection. In the absence of intimacy, our souls remain lonely and unfulfilled, no matter how busy our social lives may be. The presence of spiritual intimacy infuses everyday reality with sweetness and joy.

The word *intimate* comes from the Latin *intimus*, which means "the innermost." To be intimate with someone means to be conscious of his innermost being, to be mindful not just of what he says and does, but of the secret and sacred source from which his words and actions emanate. To be intimate means meeting the world in its depth and recognizing all beings as unique and precious emanations of Spirit.

Sadly, many people find that religion does not help them feel a sense of intimacy with God. The God they know is abstract, distant, and unapproachable. I suspect that the craving for constant stimulation and entertainment that plagues American society reflects a deep and unaddressed hunger for intimate connection—especially with the deeper Self or God. When we cultivate a personal, intimate relationship with God, we discover that God is passionate, welcoming, and very near.

If you want more ecstasy in your life, focus on intimacy. *Ecstasy is total intimacy with life.* Intimacy arises naturally when you listen deeply, not just with your ears and mind but also with your heart and soul. If you listen in this way—to yourself, to others, to trees and animals, even to rocks and streams—then your listening will naturally become a kind of prayer, a recognition of the spiritual Beloved in all things.

Some lovers of God also have human lovers. Others live celibate lives, not because they believe that God begrudges them the pleasures of sex or because they consider sexual love dirty or shameful. It's just that they already feel completely satisfied and fulfilled. This is the understanding of celibacy of which the author Thomas Moore, himself a former monastic, writes: "The monk's celibacy is not simply the absence of sex and marriage. The monk is not wedded to anything but the infinite, and that relationship is extraordinarily elusive. If you're married to All and Nothing, the Minimum and the Maximum (in Nicholas of Cusa's wording), you're a celibate in the world."[3] As Moore points out, the monk has not given up romance and intimacy—he just finds it in his relationship with the Divine.

The Ecstatic Tradition

The image of God as lover is ancient, and it permeates all religious traditions. Ecstatics revel in the imagery of sexual love because no other human experience reflects so accurately the nature of what transpires between the soul and God in the secret chambers of the heart. Since the dawn of history, mystics have celebrated this love affair between the transcendent Spirit and the incarnate human soul. "Infinity is in love with the products of time," declared the late-18th-century English poet William Blake. In the 13th century, the German mystic Mechthild of Magdeburg wrote down the words she heard God the lover speaking to her.

> *I am love itself*
> *How could I not love you passionately?*
> *I long for you to love me with all your heart,*
> *and my longing makes me love you again and again.*[4]

One of the greatest defenders of ecstatic love was Jalal ad-Din Rumi, a 13th-century Persian mystic who wrote many poems in praise of love and the drunkenness it causes. Whereas we tend to think that lovers are caught in a state of intoxication that blinds them to what we cynically call "the real world," Rumi turns the conventional view upside down. Lovers, he claims, are drunk indeed, yet far from blind. On the contrary, they, and *only* they, know the truth; they alone have penetrated the illusion of appearance. The fools are the supposedly "sane" people who frown upon the love drunks. Don't fall back into the blindness of your ordinary mindset, Rumi begs us. Keep the lover's vision alive!

> *Advice doesn't help lovers!*
> *They're not the kind of mountain stream*
> *you can build a dam across.*
> *An intellectual doesn't know*
> *what the drunk is feeling!*
> *Don't try to figure*
> *what those lost inside love*
> *will do next!*
> *Someone in charge would give up all his power,*
> *if he caught one whiff of the wine-musk*
> *from the room where the lovers*
> *are doing who-knows-what!*[5]

Rumi entices us with a vision of life lived in a state of ecstatic "in-loveness." And unlike poets who use sexual love only as a metaphor for spiritual love, Rumi sees the two as inseparable.

> *They try to say what you are, spiritual or sexual?*
> *They wonder about Solomon and all his wives.*
> *In the body of the world, they say, there is a soul*
> *and you are that.*
> *But we have ways within each other*
> *that will never be said by anyone.*[6]

What is the universe but Spirit loving itself, dancing and playing, endlessly creating itself anew? We speak of religious ecstasy and of sexual ecstasy, but ultimately, all ecstasy is of the soul, whether we find it in bed or in meditation, in nature or in creative work. Whenever we truly make love, Spirit is a participant. And whether our partner is human or divine, embodied or not, the fruit of good lovemaking is always ecstasy.

Men in Love with God

It makes sense that women might approach God as a lover, but what about men? In our tradition, the assumption that God is male is so deeply rooted that few heterosexual men would ever dream of describing their relationship with Spirit as romantic, let alone marital. A male client told me, "If I'm going to have a love affair with God, I'll have to start thinking of Him as Her. In theory, I can accept that, but in practice, it's difficult. It goes against a lifetime of conditioning."

"Well," I said, "If you can't conceive of God as feminine, then you'll have a hard time seeing the Divine within your girlfriend. So this practice might benefit your love life as well as your spirituality." At the same time, I emphasized that I was not asking him to think of God as a woman, but rather as a power that encompasses both masculine and feminine energies and wants him to feel ecstatic pleasure and joy.

We must understand that the marriage between God and the soul is not literally a heterosexual affair. Even mystics who use the heterosexual metaphor often take the liberty of switching genders, as when the Indian poet Kabir describes himself as a young woman awaiting her lover. Rumi, on the other hand, often speaks as a man in love with another man—the wandering mystic Shams ad-Din. His imagery leaves no doubt about the erotic nature of their connection.

> *At night we fall into each other with such grace.*
> *When it's light, you throw me back*
> *like you do your hair.*
> *Your eyes now drunk with God,*
> *mine with looking at you,*
> *one drunkard takes care of another.*[7]

In the end, gender dissolves and what remains is the one blazing love that encompasses and transcends all forms and variants of human love as it leaps back and forth between the two poles of human soul and infinite source.

The Implications of Taking God as Lover

When we speak of making love with God, we are using a metaphor for an experience that transcends language. A metaphor might seem an insignificant thing, a mere figure of speech, yet metaphors deeply influence how we think and act. You can expect profound shifts to occur in your life and your spirituality when you begin relating to God the lover. Here, I would just like to mention the five most important ones. They are:

- ༀ You commit to fully inhabiting your body
- ༀ You welcome pleasure as a blessing
- ༀ You become God's partner
- ༀ You become pregnant with divine light
- ༀ You commit to communicating with Spirit—for better or for worse

You Commit to Fully Inhabiting Your Body

In the San Francisco Bay area, I used to visit a large Buddhist meditation center called Spirit Rock. Every Monday night, several hundred people would gather, some sitting on pillows, others on chairs. Jack Kornfield would often lead the meditation, beginning with the words, "Find a comfortable way of sitting." Instantly, the entire hall would erupt in a flurry of bodies rearranging and resettling themselves. Every time this happened, I would think, "How strange that it doesn't occur to us to sit comfortably unless we are told to do so."

Unfortunately, patriarchal religions suffer from a profound distrust of the body and of sexuality. The great challenge of the spiritual life, we were told, was to transcend the body. Accordingly, we learned to distrust our bodies and our sexuality. We forgot that fully inhabiting our bodies—vulnerable, sensitive, and flawed as they are—takes a thousand times more courage than transcending them.

The body is a condensation of spiritual presence and provides the field within which our spiritual experience unfolds. Ecstasy, too, is experienced in and through the body. Perhaps the afterlife will bring us experiences of disembodied ecstasy. But during this life, our work lies within the physical world and within the body. Simply put, you can't make love without your body. Therefore, the path of making love with life requires us to inhabit our bodies fully, even though this means going against a great deal of cultural conditioning.

We talk about the body incessantly. We worry about it, as one might worry about an animal that appears tame, yet now and then reveals its true wildness. As a society, we obsess about our looks and spend billions of dollars on cosmetics, clothing, and cosmetic surgery. We desperately want to be slender, fit, and well-groomed. But all of this is the mind's interpretation of the body. None of it has anything to do with the body's inner life, the way it knows itself from the inside.

Our bodies possess great spiritual wisdom. They understand the diverse rhythms of the inner organs and how they relate to the rhythms of the cosmos. They understand ebb and flow, night and day, summer and winter, inhalation and exhalation. They know how to be born, how to die, and how to create new life. If you want more ecstasy in your life, listen deeply to your body and trust its guidance. Fully inhabiting your body means more than eating well and exercising regularly. It means being on intimate terms with your flesh, communicating with it, listening to it. It means getting out of your head and into your guts. Like a horse that knows the way home, even though its rider might not, your body knows what ecstasy feels like and how to get to it. It longs for ecstasy and grieves when your mind becomes so attached to control that it can't surrender to magic, playfulness, and delight.

You Welcome Pleasure as a Blessing

Most of us were raised with the metaphor of God the father, which emphasizes God's protective power. At the same time, it discourages us from contemplating God's sensuality, let alone sexuality. To even think about making love with your father is to break a deep-seated cultural taboo. There can be no question of merging or uniting with God the father. There are limits to how intimate you can get with Him. You might love Him, but you understand that you must not overstep the boundaries between yourself and God. You see, then, why those who define God as transcendent and disembodied prefer the image of God as father rather than as lover.

Our society, based as it is on Puritanism, feels ambivalent about pleasure, especially sexual pleasure. Many of us grew up with the image of an authoritarian, judgmental, punitive God who frowned upon pleasure and approved of suffering and self-denial. We want pleasure and spend a lot of time pursuing it, but we also distrust it and tend to feel ashamed of our sexual desires. Yet the connection between sex and ecstasy is natural—sex *can* give us physical ecstasy. Although physical ecstasy is limited, it is a form of ecstasy that many people have experienced and can use as a reference point. Think of the most pleasurable, intense orgasm you have ever had and imagine feeling such pleasure not just in your body but in your entire being— body, heart, and soul—and you sense what ecstasy means.

To open to God the lover is to open to the spirit of erotic pleasure and sensual enjoyment. As long as pleasure obeys the dictates of love, we should consider it an agent of healing and welcome it as a divine messenger. We're not talking about greedily racing after ever more intense sensations, but about fully welcoming the pleasures that come our way—fully tasting a ripe peach, fully receiving a warm hug, really enjoying the sight of a beautiful woman without guilt.

How do we receive pleasure? Through the senses, you may say. But this is not wholly true. You can taste something delicious without feeling much pleasure—in fact, this is what we do most of the time when we eat. The keys to receiving pleasure are *being fully present* and *breathing*. When you breathe deeply, the sensory experience has a chance to connect with the deeper core of your being—your soul, if you like. Try it and you will see that this is true. Tasting, smelling, touching, hearing, and seeing are not enough. You need to inhale each pleasurable sensation in order to fully receive it as a blessing.

You Become God's Partner

God the father promises protection, compassion, and security. When God becomes our Mother, a greater element of nurturing intimacy enters our conception of the Divine. Still, so long as you envision God as a parent, you are in a hierarchical relationship in which the Divine has all the power.

Some would say that the soul chooses its parents, but for all practical purposes, children get the parents they get and have to make the best of it. But we *do* choose our lovers. So when you call upon God as your lover, you acknowledge that you are in this relationship by choice, and you envision a balanced partnership.

Making love involves reciprocity, choice, desire, intimacy, co-creation, and responsibility. The image of God as lover opens our minds to the startling possibility that God's desire for us might match our desire for the Divine. Instead of feeling like insignificant insects crawling toward a giant, we claim our equality with the Divine—equality not in power, but in our essential nature. Just as a drop of ocean water shares the ocean's essence, we share God's essence.

Making love with God implies give and take—even some need or vulnerability on God's part. A spiritual love affair is always a two-way street. "I desired you before the world began," Mechthild of Magdeburg heard God saying to her soul.

> *I desire you now,*
> *Even as you desire me.*
> *Where our two desires become as one,*
> *There love's longing is fulfilled.*[8]

Just as we all long to be loved totally, God longs to be loved totally. Men and women in love with God know this. They feel not only their desire for God, but also God's desire for them. Even times of estrangement and struggle serve to strengthen their bond with Spirit.

Although we may be God's creatures, we are also God's partners in an ongoing creative adventure. This invests us with tremendous power and responsibility. If we don't like the way things are going in the world, we cannot simply blame God, any more than a disgruntled husband or wife can blame a spouse for the failure of the marriage. We must take responsibility for our part. We have the power to do both good and evil, and our actions make a difference. By defining ourselves as God's lovers, we acknowledge and accept our responsibility for the world.

You Become Pregnant with Divine Light

Like a woman ready to conceive, the soul realizes her fertility and her full creative power when she takes God as her lover. We understand, then, that the cosmos is not a finished project but rather an unfolding work of art that we are co-creating with God. We are, in fact, already pregnant—pregnant with the future, which is born of the meeting between God's desire and our own.

When the Holy Spirit made love with Mary, she became the Mother of God. All around the world we find stories of divine children—Jesus, Krishna, the Buddha, Durga—born to human parents who made love with God. When we dismiss such stories as having no bearing on our own lives, we miss their true message. As the medieval German mystic Meister Eckhart pointed out, all human beings are called to be mothers of God—men and women alike. All who make love with Spirit will conceive and become pregnant with an otherworldly joy. They will nurture a pure, innocent, and unsullied spirit that radiates divine love into the world, and they will give birth to acts of compassion and beauty.

Many western psychotherapists offer "inner child" work. We must understand, however, that healing the wounds of childhood is not an end in itself, but only a preliminary step toward uncovering the pure light of the divine child within—our luminous, pure, ecstatic Self. That divine child within each of us is both the source of ecstasy and the innocent purity of our true nature.

You Commit to Communicating with Spirit—for Better or for Worse

A relationship is like a house built of a million bricks, each one an act of communication. Couples give each other gifts, prepare meals for each other, plan vacations. They talk, argue, fight, make up, make love. They tell stories, laugh, play, joke, explain, question, interpret. They relate face-to-face, on the phone, through letters, through e-mail. When communication breaks down, so does the relationship.

Our marriage with Spirit, too, requires regular communication. We pray, dance, laugh, cry, light candles. We create beauty, practice compassion, read spiritual literature. We know the Divine by the beauty we see in a child's face and by the love we feel in our hearts. Throughout the day, we stay engaged in an ongoing dialogue with the Divine.

Communication is not difficult when relationships are loving and harmonious. But what about when conflicts arise? The strongest, most vibrant marriages are usually those between men and women who know how to fight well, who speak their truth clearly yet respectfully, and who do not cave in easily. In fact, fighting is sometimes the surest sign of intimacy.

In our marriage with Spirit, too, we need to know how to fight. When bad things happen to us, we must find a way to direct our anger and our sense of injustice toward Spirit. Otherwise, we'll withdraw and turn bitter and cynical. Our passion for life and our ability to be intimate with each moment will diminish, and we'll lose our capacity for ecstasy.

All the great mystics argued ferociously with Spirit. Tukaram, an Indian mystic born in 1608, railed at the God to whose service he had devoted his entire life.

I'll fight
You
And I'm sure
I'll hit you
In the tenderest spot.

Lord
You are a lizard
A toad
And a tiger
Too

And at times
You are
a coward
Frantically
Covering
Your own arse

When you face
A stronger-willed
Assault
You just
Turn tail
You attack
Only the weak
Who
Try to run away

Says Tuka
Get
Out of my way

You are
Neither man
Nor woman
You aren't even
A thing.[9]

But this is not the end of the story. Tukaram's struggles with God are like the fights that occur within every marriage—they pass; anger dissolves and gives way to love. In Tukaram's later poems, it is evident that the turbulence has passed. "I wear the jewels of pure joy," he cries. "I rock to the ecstatic beat of freedom."[10] More and more, his poems become stammerings of joy that trail off into an amazed silence.

Were you taught to think of God as an easily angered boss whom you needed to handle with kid gloves? If your God is primarily an authority figure, you probably don't talk to Spirit with the same freedom and intimacy with which you talk to your lover. You may not realize that sometimes the only way to honor your spiritual passion is to yell and fight and argue with God. If you withdraw instead of communicating your feelings of anger, pain, or fear, your relationship with God will wither and die as surely as any marriage would.

The Biblical figure of Job presents us with a wonderful role model of someone who felt wronged by God and took up the fight. His friends all told him to back down. "God is just," they said. "You must have provoked God's anger. Ask for forgiveness." Job shook his head. "I'm innocent," he said. "God is torturing me, and I am going to hold Him accountable." In the end, Job's perseverance paid off. God revealed Himself to Job. Although Job's questions were never answered in any linear, conceptual way, the sight of God gave Job something far more valuable than rational understanding—reverence, devotion, and awe. Having met God face-to-face, Job recovered his inner peace.

Often, people don't realize that they are going through a spiritual

TRY THIS...

Sit down with pen and paper. Close your eyes for a few minutes. Breathe, and invite God to be present with you.

Now, imagine that God wants to write you a love letter, but needs you to be the scribe. So you must write down whatever you hear God saying in the silence of your listening heart.

What does God see in you? Why has God fallen in love with you? Why has God chosen you as lover? Let God answer these questions.

Don't let shame, embarrassment, or false modesty get in your way. Write down whatever you hear. Give God a chance to express love for you.

---

crisis when they cannot let go of anger and resentment. They don't understand that their marriage to Spirit is on the rocks. They only know that they feel bitter. And because they can't change the past, they feel stuck.

If you are in this position, your first step is to acknowledge that you are angry with God. By acknowledging your anger, you invite a dialogue. Your love affair with God operates on the same principles as any human love affair. When you're angry, you had better talk about it; otherwise the unexpressed anger will undermine the relationship.

Love Affair or Marriage?

My first experience of making love with Spirit occurred when I was 4 or 5 years old. I was playing with my friends in a garden strewn with spring wildflowers—yellow, white, purple, and brilliant poppy orange. Squealing with delight, we chased each other across the sweet-smelling grass, tumbling over each other like puppies and becoming more and more excited. Suddenly, I found myself lying on the grass looking up into the sky. Everything around me had become silent and immense, as if the whole universe were holding its breath. Everything, I realized in that moment, was made of light—the trees, the grass, my own body—and everything was quivering with joy. For a brief moment, I knew that everything in the universe was alive and conscious. Then the moment passed—I heard my friends' shrill voices, and our play continued.

Many people have had similar moments of ecstasy. For some, however, such fortuitous encounters with Spirit aren't enough. Their souls' hunger drives them to a deeper commitment—a marriage of sorts. This "marriage" might be a spiritual dedication that grows spontaneously, or it might require a more formal ritual, such as those the ancient Indian temple dancers performed. My friend Jeff's marriage to Spirit took the form of a spontaneous vow.

> When I was 26 years old, I spent a month meditating at a Zen monastery. Behind the monastery was a hill that I used to climb in the early evening. One evening, I was sitting at the top of the hill looking out over the valley. Suddenly, everything in me went completely silent. My whole being became crystal clear and absolutely still and alert. Then, in the midst of this stillness, joy started welling up. This joy just kept intensifying until I could hardly bear it. I looked at the trees and the sky and the rocks, and I was weeping with love and with gratitude.
>
> And then, without a thought in my mind, yet from a place of total certainty and knowing, I spoke to the Spirit of the universe and I dedicated the rest of my life to its service and to the service of love. That vow has re-

mained the foundation of my life. I didn't plan it, it just happened. Nonetheless, it was as real and binding a commitment as you can imagine.

In most spiritual marriages, people experience a sense of being called and of responding. They choose God, but they also sense that God has chosen them. Slowly, over the years, the relationship grows and deepens.

Sometimes, however, God seems to pounce on people, ravishing them and overwhelming them with ecstasy. The marriage is consummated in a flash, with no time to question, deliberate, or withdraw. God enters their being and unites with them in such a way that from that moment on, they are radically transformed.

Such was the experience of the famous Inuit shaman Uvavnuk. One day Uvavnuk was outdoors when a ball of heavenly fire descended and lodged itself within her body. With this light blazing within her, she came running into her home, singing the song that, from that moment on, became her main healing song. According to witness accounts,

> As soon as she began to sing, she became delirious with joy and all the others in the house also were beyond themselves with joy, because their minds were being cleansed of all that burdened them. They lifted up their arms and cast away everything connected with suspicion and malice. All these things one could blow away like a speck of dust from the palm of the hand with this song:

> *The great sea has set me in motion,*
> *Set me adrift,*
> *Moving me as the weed moves in a river*
> *The arch of sky and mightiness of storms*

TRY THIS...

Dialoguing with God is not as difficult as you might think. The main thing required is receptivity. You have to be willing to really listen. And since God's voice is usually subtle and quiet (a "still, small voice"), you'll need to listen with total attention, putting your own thoughts and ideas aside.

Sit down with pen and paper. Spend a few minutes breathing deeply and settling down. Now, write down a question you want to ask God.

Then, switch the pen to your nondominant hand. If you are right-handed, switch to your left hand. If you are left-handed, switch to your right hand. As you switch, mentally affirm that you are giving over this second hand as an instrument through which God can write.

Instead of thinking about your question, be as receptive as you can to the voice of Spirit and write down whatever you hear. Continue writing until you feel a sense of completeness.

Writing with your nondominant hand may feel awkward and childlike. That's all right—the voice of truth is usually simple and straightforward. Moreover, writing with your nondominant hand forces you to slow down, which enhances your receptivity.

Have moved the spirit within me,
Till I am carried away
Trembling with joy.[11]

From this moment on, Uvavnuk was transformed. Having become a powerful shaman and healer, she lived in service to her community and to the ecstatic Spirit that inspired her song.

Naturally, you may wonder whether you are really hearing the voice of Spirit or just writing down thoughts. Put that question aside for now. Approach this exercise as sacred play. Hearing the voice of Spirit takes practice—the more you do it, the easier it gets. You can't practice as long as your inner critic is looking over your shoulder, accusing you of being inauthentic, naïve, or deluded. Give yourself permission to experiment. Assume that God will take the opportunity to communicate with you.

Switch back to your first hand and, as you do so, feel yourself returning to your ordinary sense of self. Consider what Spirit said to you, and then voice your objections, your questions, your confusion—just as you would in an ordinary conversation. Did God's response completely answer your question? Did it raise new questions? Using your dominant hand, write down whatever you are thinking at this point.

You have begun your dialogue with Spirit. Continue this dialogue until the conversation feels complete. Know that you can resume it at any time.

You can vary this practice by using only your dominant hand, speaking the dialogue out loud, or merely allowing it to unfold silently within your mind.

Translating It into Everyday Life

As the author and teacher A. H. Almaas points out, the concept of making love with God bewilders the mind. We are used to having a specific object to love—a person, an animal, a thing. How can we make love with something that is by definition no-thing—vast and undefinable? A lover in the spiritual sense, says Almaas, "is someone

(continued on page 34)

TRY THIS...

I assure you that you can learn to make love with life, because that is what you were born to do. Here is an exercise I sometimes teach in workshops. Its purpose is to help you gain a sense of what making love with life might mean to you personally.

Take a piece of paper and a pen and ask yourself: What, in my experience, are the most important ingredients of great lovemaking? Make a list. Each person's list will be somewhat different and may change over time. My most recent list has nine points:

1. I'm totally present and fully engaged. I'm not thinking about what I should have said to a client yesterday, nor am I planning tonight's dinner.

2. Love is my highest priority. I'll do whatever intensifies the feelings of love between my partner and myself, and I'll avoid doing anything that would diminish this love.

3. I'm equally open to giving and to receiving pleasure.

4. My whole body is involved and all my senses are awake. I'm touching, smelling, tasting, looking, feeling, and listening.

5. I am without shame. I love and accept my own body just the way it is, and I accept my partner's body just the way it is.

6. I allow myself to be vulnerable. I hide neither my body nor my emotional and spiritual responses. I allow my partner to see me in the most intimate ways.

7. I'm at play, open to whatever presents itself. I allow myself to be spontaneous, creative, funny, and experimental.

8. I'm open to learning new things about myself and my partner.

9. I trust in the goodness of where my body is leading me. I surrender to the process.

Notice that I describe my behavior as a fact, rather than as a wish or an idea. That is, instead of saying, "I would like to be totally present," or "I wish I were totally present," I say, "I am totally present." This sends a strong message to the psyche that I fully intend and expect to live this statement.

Before you read any further, stop and make your own list, based on your personal experience of what is involved in good lovemaking. Remember that you can always add to or change your list later.

Now read your list again. This time, assume that *the same attitudes and behaviors that work in bed will also work in life.* Take a new piece of paper, go to the first point, and describe in as much detail as possible what that point would mean to you in the context of making love with life.

Again, let me use my own list as an example. After rereading my first point, I wrote, "I am totally present and fully engaged. Even if what I'm doing is as mundane as changing a light bulb or filling a prescription at the pharmacy, I give it my undivided attention. I honor the present moment as the most important and sacred of my entire life."

Now, explore how the statement you have just written challenges you to change. For example, I noted: "I'm rarely present when I drive. I don't like driving, so I'm not sure I want to be present. If I spend an

(continued)

TRY THIS ... (CONT.)

hour a day in my car, that's 365 hours a year—more than 15 days! How can I make driving a sacred experience? I am going to try choosing some tapes to listen to, or a mantra or an affirmation to work with, before I leave the house. If I want to use driving time to think about things, that's fine, but I would like to be more conscious of making that choice."

It's up to you how deeply you want to explore each point on your list. One of my clients had twelve points on her list, and she decided to devote an entire year to meditating on them, devoting a month to each point. Every morning she would recall the element of good lovemaking to which that month was dedicated, and throughout the day she tried to put her insights into practice.

By the end of the year, she was amazed at how much her life had changed—outwardly and especially inwardly. "I'm a much happier person than I used to be. People have been commenting on it. I feel as though an inner light has been switched on and I'm shining. I feel shy about saying this, but I've fallen in love with my life. It's just an ordinary, messed-up life, but it's mine, and I am learning to really love it."

who is personal with God, personal with Being, with essence. The only way you could be personal with God is through love—by being a lover. This is the only way. And that is the true essence of what a lover is—being personal with the universal. . . . It's a difficult concept to grasp. The mind can't grasp it. It doesn't make sense. We are saying that two categories that don't go together actually exist inseparably in the lover; it defies all rules of logic. 'I've never experienced anything like that. It's not possible.' But love makes it possible. You could be completely in love with the universal, with everything, with the totality. Then you are a true lover."[12]

More than just a concept, becoming God's lover is a path and, above all, an ongoing practice—the most challenging, subtle, and rewarding one you'll ever undertake. We sometimes assume that making love is something we don't need to learn. We are supposed to know how to do it without having to learn or practice. In fact, good lovemaking—whether physical or spiritual—is an art that requires tremendous skill. Like all arts, it must be practiced, honed, and refined.

CHAPTER TWO

The Dance
of the Great Hunger

I played for ten years with the girls my own age,
but now I am suddenly in fear.
I am on the way up some stairs—they are high.
Yet I have to give up my fears
if I want to take part in this love.

I have to let go the protective clothes
and meet him with the whole length of my body.
My eyes will have to be the love-candles this time.
Kabir says: Men and women in love will understand this poem.
If what you feel for the Holy One is not desire,
then what's the use of dressing with such care,
and spending so much time making your eyelids dark?

—Kabir

We sometimes think of saints and mystics as people who have renounced desire. In fact, nothing could be further from the truth. All the great mystics, from the German Meister Eckhart to the Persian Rumi, have been pleasure seekers of the most discriminating and demanding kind. However, the ordinary pleasures of daily life—good food, sex, wealth, and fame—did not satisfy them. They wanted more—a greater ecstasy, a wilder abandon, a deeper joy. Their capacity for pleasure was so immense that nothing less than union with the Infinite could satiate their hunger.

When people wondered why the 16th-century Indian poet Mirabai chose to make love with Spirit and rejected all human lovers, she laughingly responded, "I have felt the swaying of the elephant's shoulders . . . and now you

In the spiritual realm, hunger and satisfaction are not necessarily opposites; they interweave in mysterious ways.

want me to climb on a jackass? Try to be serious!"[1]

Mirabai didn't despise worldly pleasures—it was just that deep within her soul, she had found a love so passionate and so consuming that it eclipsed all lesser loves. For the sake of this love, Mirabai burned in the fire of her desire for God the lover. "The pain of his absence burns my bewildered heart and gives me no rest," she cried in one of her songs.[2] Many of her poems are like the screams of a birthing woman, full of a raw, wild intensity—yet out of that pain is born the amazing rapture that illuminates her words.

Babies are born screaming with hunger; the absence of hunger signals death. Yet hunger is a strange thing: We want to feel it—nothing else makes us feel quite so alive—but we also want to get rid of it because it is uncomfortable, even painful. Hunger makes us feel incomplete, discontent, and less than whole. A gaping hole has opened within us, and our impulse is to fill that hole as quickly as possible.

When we get what we want, our anguish evaporates—but so does the delicious alertness we felt previously. It seems that we have to choose between two evils: We are either hungry but fully alive or satiated but drowsy. Certainly, physical hunger knows only two possibilities—hunger or satiety.

In the spiritual realm, however, different laws apply. There, hunger and satisfaction are not necessarily opposites; they interweave in mysterious ways. The hunger for ecstasy is like a question that contains its own answer. The more you feel it, the more you realize that within the hunger itself lies a kernel of raw, wild rapture. Instead of extinguishing our hunger, ecstasy fans its flames to a white-hot intensity, uniting the apparent opposites of intense desire and equally intense satisfaction. Ecstasy, whether we find it in love, nature, spiritual practice, or creative work, takes us to an edge where intense longing merges with intense pleasure. To reach that edge, however, we need the courage to feel our hunger in all its ravenous intensity *without running away.*

The most beautiful celebration of the hunger for ecstasy I have come across is from the African continent. In a book about the Kalahari bushmen, Laurens van der Post describes two dances, the "dance of the little hunger" and the "dance of the great hunger." The dance of the little hunger "is of the physical hunger the child experiences the moment he is born and satisfies first at his mother's breast, and which from then on stays with him for the rest of his life on earth. But the second dance is the dance of a hunger that neither the food of the earth nor the way of life possible upon it can satisfy. It is a dance of the Bushman's instinctive intimation that man cannot live by bread alone, although without it he cannot live at all; hence the two."[3]

Van der Post goes on to describe how, in the dance of the great hunger, the dancer throws his head back and raises his eyes with an expression of immense longing, with "his hands stretched as high as they could, palms wide open, fingertips trembling as if he were pleading, begging, praying to something high up beyond his and our vision." Despite their convoluted language, the bushmen's message is clear: "Whenever I asked them about this great hunger they would only say, 'not only we dancing, feeling ourselves to be raising the dust which will one day come blown by the wind to erase our last spoor from the sand when we die, lest others coming and seeing our footsteps there might still think us alive, not only we feel this hunger, but the stars too, sitting up there with their hearts of plenty, they too feel it and feeling it, tremble as if afraid they would wane and their light die, on account of so great a hunger.'"[4]

These people understand that our hunger for ecstasy is not a problem demanding a solution, but a sacred force humming with intense energy and vitality. Our task is not to get rid of this hunger, as if it were a disease, but to welcome it as a guide along our path. It is here to stay and is, in fact, as much a sign of health as our appetite for physical food is. Although it causes us to suffer, it also keeps us alive and holds the key to ecstasy.

If the "great hunger" is to serve as our guide, we must hold it sacred. To hold desire sacred means to see it as a pathway to the Divine, springing from the eternal attraction between God and the soul. Just as physical hunger drives a tiger to hunt, the great hunger impels us to stalk more elusive prey—the nameless, invisible source of all ecstasy. Our hunger for ecstasy deserves to be held sacred. It is the magnet that attracts us to God, the fuel that drives the spiritual quest, and the compelling force behind our immense appetite for life, love, and adventure.

Desire Is Not a Spiritual Hindrance

Lotus blossoms look like purity incarnate as they rock gently to and fro on the dark waters of a lake. At night, when their delicate, luminous petals shimmer mysteriously in the silvery moonlight, they radiate an otherworldly beauty, as if they were angelic presences that might dissolve at the touch of a human hand. Yet lotus plants actually have strong, tenacious roots that anchor them in the mud of the lake bottom.

Like a lotus, ecstasy seems too beautiful to be real. It seems like a taste of paradise or like an angel's kiss. Such joy cannot possibly be of this world—but it is. Ecstasy is as firmly rooted in physical nature as a lotus plant. Our flesh and blood provide the soil ecstasy thrives in—if you chop off the flower from its root, it will die.

Unfortunately, chopping off the flower from its root is precisely what many people assume spirituality means. They approach the body, with all its needs and desires, as a hindrance rather than as the rich, muddy soil in which lotuses thrive. They might want the spectacular blossoms of ecstatic joy, but the slimy roots embarrass them, so they hide those roots, bury them, pretend they don't exist. They equate spirituality with denial of their physicality. Transcendence then becomes a euphemism for ignorance, repression, and denial.

If it had no desire to feel the warming touch of the sunlight on its petals, the lotus would never grow toward the surface of the pond. Desire is a powerful, life-affirming force. Nonetheless, many religious traditions disapprove of desire for a wide variety of reasons. People who pursue their desires are often called selfish and are compared unfavorably with the "selfless" ones who have no wants and needs of their own. Desire—especially the desire for sensual pleasure—is often viewed as a force that lures us away from God.

Other religious teachings simply dismiss the pursuit of pleasure as a waste of time. The delights we chase after, they say, are as impermanent as clouds. Worse still, the fulfillment of your desires may actually bring you further suffering. You get the new car you wanted, and then someone dents your shiny new toy and you're depressed for days. We've all experienced some variant of this story; we can all attest to the truth of the Buddha's teaching that attachment is the root cause of all suffering. We suffer, in other words, because often things don't turn out the way we want.

Nonetheless, I wholeheartedly disagree with those who condemn desire as an obstacle to spiritual evolution. In my opinion, advising people to renounce their desires does them a serious disservice. First, it simply doesn't work. I have witnessed at least a dozen spiritual organizations destroyed by sexual scandal. In every case, those involved were desperately maintaining the pretense of having transcended desire. Wherever desire is scorned, hypocrisy and deceit abound.

Moreover, in rejecting desire, we reject one of our greatest spiritual teachers. My own experience has convinced me that if you follow your desire, it will take you on a journey, in the course of which you will gain immense wisdom, strength, and compassion.

The Journey Home

When our desire seems to emanate from the very depths of the soul, we should go after what we want—not because its fulfillment will necessarily make us happy, but because in the process, we will grow and learn and expand in ways we would not if we tried to squelch desire.

For example, I desired the home I now live in for a long time before I found it. For years, I prayed and searched. I drove thousands of miles, my heart pounding hopefully as I entered each new potential hometown. Every time I had to cross off a town from my list of candidates, my heart sank in disappointment.

In the meantime, I meditated with my local Buddhist community and listened to lectures on the virtue of detachment. All suffering, the Buddha taught, can be traced back to the dilemma of wanting this and rejecting that—attachment and aversion. Give up all preferences, he advised. If you accept what you have, you will be happy.

I did, in fact, learn to be happy where I was and to appreciate the blessings that surrounded me, but the yearning in my heart never abated. In fact, as the years went by, I wanted a true home more than ever. "If you were more evolved," I told myself, "you would let go of this need. Don't you know home is an inner place?" My desire shrugged. It had a life of its own and didn't care what I said.

Eventually, I found my home—a log cabin, as it turned out. On sunny mornings, the cedar logs seem to glow with their own golden light, and on cold winter days, they cradle me in their warm, comforting embrace. Every day I give thanks for the spaciousness, tranquillity, and beauty of my home. I still have good days and bad days, but when I'm happy, my happiness is fuller than ever before. More of me is present, as if the texture of my being had become richer. Having persistently begged and prayed and searched for the thing I wanted, and having finally had my desire satisfied, I now feel loved by Spirit more deeply than ever before.

Moreover, I am no longer the same person who first acknowledged her desire. The process of seeking satisfaction has changed me. It taught me a great deal about my true nature and my needs. It forced me to make big commitments and challenged me to leap into the unknown. It honed my intuition and deepened my sense of mystery. I cannot help but conclude that desire has served as my teacher. It has led me on a path that, like any true path, has transformed me.

Buddhism and Desire

Patriarchal religions tend to reject desire as a spiritual hindrance. The flavor of that rejection, however, differs from East to West. Most Christian teachings view God and the world as separate and insist that the seeker must choose between God and the world. Worldly and spiritual desires are considered incompatible.

Buddhism appeals to disillusioned Western seekers precisely because it does not view the physical world as antithetical to the spiritual. Nonetheless, Buddhism has its own brand of puritanism. Many Buddhists frown upon sensuality and passion, and issue emphatic warnings against getting carried away by desire.

One of the most important goals of Buddhist practice is to live fully in the present moment without attempting to alter, improve, or escape it. As Pema Chödrön, an American Buddhist nun and teacher, points out, "Whether you get meditation instruction from the Theravada tradition or the Zen tradition or the Vajrayana tradition, the basic instruction is always about being awake in the present moment."[5]

Desire is suspect to Buddhists because of its tendency to pull us out of the present moment and get us tangled in a vortex of fantasies about what could or should or might be. Chödrön advises us that instead of indulging in

The creative dance of desire is essential to our nature and deserves a place of honor in our spiritual practice.

dreams of a better future, we should "abandon any hope of fruition."[6] By this she means that we should make peace with the imperfection of things rather than clinging to the hope that in the future everything will be perfect—we'll be 20 pounds lighter, our sex lives will be great, and we'll be enlightened. That's not going to happen, she assures us. Things get better and they get worse, but they will never be perfect, so stop banking on the future and start living in the present.

This is good advice. Our failure to make peace with what is *does* cause us to suffer. Most of us are light years removed from living in the present and could benefit from 10 years or so in a Buddhist monastery. We cause ourselves much unnecessary pain by demanding that this world be a paradise, which it is not and never will be.

But what is the present moment? Is it like a room that we step into? Or is it more like a construction site that awaits our creative input? I suspect it is the latter. The present moment doesn't arrive ready-made and complete. It's not a finished product but rather something we create in conjunction with life, moment by moment. What exactly we create depends in large measure on how deeply we honor our desires and hopes.

As a predominantly monastic path, Buddhism naturally distrusts the power of desire. Yet to consistently resist the future-oriented thrust of desire is to suppress an important manifestation of our creativity. In every moment, the real and the possible dance together within the ground of our being, and out of this dance the future is born. This creative dance of desire is essential to our nature and deserves to be given a place of honor within our spiritual practice. When we honor desire, sparks fly and we burn like candles on the altar of life.

As ecstatics, we are like tightrope walkers, trying to maintain a difficult balance. On the one hand, we commit to the practice of presence in order to avoid falling into the chasm of unconsciousness. On the other hand, we make space for the inherently future-oriented thrust of our desires. We value the capacity of our creative imagination to imagine something that does not yet exist and to make it real. Instead of dismissing desire and hope as energies that pull us out of the present, we honor them as forces that help create the future.

If we go after what we want, things won't necessarily end up better than before. But provided that we approach our desires with a certain degree of consciousness, we ourselves will be better—wiser, that is, and more mature.

The Collector

I recently heard a true story about a man whose desire led him on an extraordinary journey and transformed his life in ways he would never have imagined in his wildest dreams.

This man, a construction worker, had always collected sports memorabilia, but at some point he became bored with his collection. "Why don't you collect books about Lewis and Clark?" a friend suggested. The man knew nothing about Lewis and Clark, but he went to his local book dealer and purchased an old two-volume set of their diaries. Then he went to a book expert, showed him the set, and asked whether there was anything else available. The book expert laughed so hard he almost fell off his chair, because the literature on Lewis and Clark is so vast. He laughed even more when our hero announced that he intended to have the greatest collection of Lewis and Clark literature in the United States.

The collector was not wealthy, but collecting these books became his greatest passion. He began working 10 to 12 hours a day, six and sometimes seven days a week, to finance his book collection. He refinanced his house three times and maxed out 12 credit cards. Every spare penny, and some that weren't really spare at all, went to purchase books on Lewis and Clark. He never read the books; he just wanted to own them.

After 14 years, he owned the most complete collection in the United States, including an 1814 first edition of the Lewis and Clark journals, the crown jewel of his collection, for which he had paid a whopping $12,500.

Owning the books was no longer his greatest desire, however. At some point in those last years, he had started to read the books he purchased, and the more he read, the more excited he became. His favorite part was when Lewis and Clark first saw the Pacific Ocean and noted in their journal: "Ocean in view—oh, the joy!" He sensed a kinship between his own quest to own the greatest Lewis and Clark collection and their quest to reach the ocean. Their determination, their success, and their joy mirrored his own. You could tell by the way he talked about the Pacific Ocean and about what Lewis and Clark must have felt when they saw it for the first time that, consciously or unconsciously, he recognized the ocean as his own image of ecstasy. For him, it was the symbol of fulfillment, of having reached life's ultimate destination.

In the late 1990s, the demand for Lewis and Clark literature exploded and the value of the man's collection skyrocketed. Today, he is very happily retired, having sold his collection for a small fortune when he was 54 years old. Every day, he gets up, has a leisurely breakfast, and then heads for the national Lewis and Clark library, where he spends his day reading and researching. His astonishment and delight are evident as he proudly says, "I used to be a manual laborer. Now, I have become a scholar."

The Hierarchy of Desires

If we would adopt desire as a spiritual teacher, we must first understand that not all desires are equal. Some are more aligned with the will of the soul, some less so. Often, one desire conflicts with another, forcing us to clarify our priorities. A tired father may chose to play with his children even though he longs to take a nap. A woman might have a crush on an officemate but choose not to act on it out of consideration for her husband. The pleasure of the heart runs deeper than the pleasures of the thinking mind and of the senses.

Honoring our true desires and dedicating ourselves to realizing them are not selfishness; on the contrary, these practices awaken a beautiful generosity in our hearts. The theologian Brian Swimme writes, "Our deepest desire is to share our riches, and this desire is rooted in the dynamics of the cosmos. What began as the outward expansion of the universe in the fireball ripens into your desire to flood all things with goodness. Whenever you are filled with a desire to fling your gifts into the world, you have become this cosmic dynamic of celebration, feeling its urgency to pour forth just as the stars felt the same urgency to pour themselves out."[7]

Many of us learned to censor our desires at a young age. Perhaps we were shamed for wanting so much, for wanting the "wrong" things, or for not being the quiet, grateful, undemanding children our parents wanted. If we believe that our desires are bad, selfish, or irrelevant, we will repress the awareness of the things that really make us happy—spending time with a loved one, listening to a birdsong at dawn, lying in a fragrant meadow, puttering around in the attic. We won't admit desires that might rock the boat and make us the target of criticism or anger. Maybe you want to tell your in-laws *not* to come for a week-long visit. Maybe you want not to rescue your son who just called to say that he ran out of gas for the third time this month.

If we believe that our desires are selfish, we will repress awareness of what makes us happy.

All too often, we replace our true desires with the desire to please or to fit in, and we do whatever will win us approval. We sacrifice pleasure to survival, fearing our friends and family will reject and abandon us if we dare to take our own desires seriously. Maybe they will, but whose life is it? Ours or theirs?

Desire is never good or bad—it simply is. The question is: How are we using that energy? Desire is like a servant who easily gets confused. Desire is supposed to take orders from the soul, but often it gets sidetracked into serving the ego-mind. The mind is easily misled. It is easily convinced that a red sports car, a perfect wardrobe, or a slim body are the keys to perfect happiness. Immoral behavior occurs when people fall asleep to the hunger of their souls, and instead follow the lead of superficial ego desires. Healthy morality does not ask us to renounce pleasure. It merely asks us to make our first priority the pleasure of the soul, which is always deeper, truer, and more compassionate than the pleasure of the ego. Sleeping with your spouse's best friend might be sexually pleasurable, but it certainly will not please your soul.

So the question we need to ask ourselves is: Which master do our desires serve? As we consciously work with the energy of desire, we learn to discriminate, to notice when desire has stopped serving the soul, and to steer it back on course. As the author Sam Keen says, "You must go deeper and deeper. In an incarnate or a creation kind of spirituality, we must believe that what we most deeply desire is the path of revelation, moving us beyond the illusion of needing things to fulfill us."[8]

I was 17 years old when I first discovered that different desires could pull in opposite directions. My friend Brigitte and I had gone to Greece to see the wonders of the ancient Greek civilization. We saw them and were impressed. But what impressed us even more was our Greek tour guide, a handsome young charmer who had our whole busload of tourists laughing so hard that we forgot to be terrified as we sped along the narrow mountain roads. We knew that God had a sense of humor when we found out that the man's name was Plato. We caught Plato's eye, and in no time at all, both Brigitte and I were swooning over him. Kissing him in an olive grove, my knees buckled and left me trembling like a newborn foal.

One evening, after a few days of this, Brigitte and I sat on the edge of our hotel beds and talked. It was clear that Plato wanted us. He wanted me, he wanted her, he wanted either one of us. But late that night, we had an important realization. When each of us imagined going off for a fling with Plato, leaving the other behind, we knew it would destroy our friendship. And despite our raging teenage hormones, we both knew that the fling was not worth it. The next day, we said our regretful goodbyes to Plato and took a plane to one of the other beautiful Greek islands. It still makes me happy that we had the wisdom to make that choice. I think of it as a time when two women sat together and intuitively understood the meaning of sisterhood.

The deepest desire of the human soul is to live in the ecstasy of love; all other desires are rooted in this one. Yet though the soul knows what it wants, it cannot function in the world on its own. It needs the mind to look around, gather impressions, interpret them, and choose a plan of action.

Unfortunately, the mind is riddled with confusion and ignorance. It sometimes gets programmed with false beliefs. It jumps to conclusions based on limited or faulty evidence. It doesn't understand that what worked for us when we were 5 years old doesn't necessarily work now.

Many souls are like ships steered by crazy captains. The soul whispers, "Give me ecstasy," and the captain goes and gets some cocaine. The soul whispers, "Give me ecstasy," and the captain grabs the next attractive woman who sails by.

No wonder many of us conclude that desire is a bad thing. How many times, when we've felt our souls tugging at our hearts like hungry children, have we ignored the soul, told it to shut up and go away? How many times have we repressed our wants and desires and pushed them away? But repression hasn't made us happy. We're not really contented, we're just making do, trying to settle for what is available.

Ecstasy is a lightening bolt of brilliance and power far beyond our control. No wonder it scares us. How can we trust such a power, unless we know it as a servant of the highest good? If ecstasy is anything less than God's angel, we cannot surrender to it.

Therefore, we must look carefully at the pleasures we crave. If what we desire has the potential to do harm, then it is not an expression of pure love and it won't bring true ecstasy. It's a mirage, not the true thing. Don't get hooked on the illusion. For some people, the mirage looks like a cigarette or a drink or a syringe full of heroin. Other illusions are not so easy to spot. The mirage could look like a need to have a fit, slender body. It could look like having a particular lover, standard of living, or item of clothing we think we absolutely must have. The way to see through all the disguises is to ask yourself whether your desire springs from pure love. If not, then its pursuit will not bring you closer to union with God.

The key is not to repress your desires, but to accept the challenge they present. We must dig beneath the superficial wants to find out what the deepest desire is and then ask ourselves how to satisfy that deepest desire. The answers we formulate may be clouded by our ignorance and inexperience. Still, we must act on the deepest inner knowing to which we have access at the moment. And we must follow through on our insights, even though it may mean transforming our entire way of life.

If your mind is wise, clear, and aligned with the higher dimensions, your choices will bring you happiness; if your mind is clouded by prejudice and error, they won't. Even if the outcome of your actions is not what you anticipated and does not make you happy, you can count on one thing: If you approach desire as a teacher, you will never fail to gain wisdom, compassion, and insight.

As nature has an inherent will to evolve, so do we. We are born with an innate desire for personal growth and spiritual evolution. As we evolve, so do our desires. The pleasures that once satisfied us no longer do so. Once we awaken to the soul's hunger for spiritual nourishment, physical and emotional food no longer s uffice.

Into what are we evolving, then? The medieval German mystic Meister Eckhart summed it up succinctly. Just as an acorn cannot grow into anything but an oak tree, he said, a human being is a God-seed and cannot grow into anything but God. We are God-seeds in the process of sprouting, growing, and bearing fruit. If God is ecstasy, then our hunger for ecstasy is the hunger not only to know God, but to *become* God. In other words, our desire is an expression of our soul's evolutionary drive.

Ask and You Shall Receive

The way we consciously claim our desire as an energy that propels us toward greater joy and fulfillment is by asking for what we want. You might call it prayer, but this type of prayer does not require you to be religious or even to believe in God. Prayer need not be a verbal activity. Sometimes we need to dance our prayers, like the bushmen of the Kalahari, letting our bodies move with the in-

TRY THIS...

Before a desire can be satisfied, you must feel it and become fully aware of it. Ask yourself: What do I really want? What is my true desire? What is my path to ecstasy? Contemplate these questions. Make lists of all your desires, from the most superficial to the most profound, and begin the work of sorting your desires into those of the ego and those of the soul. Accept no easy answers. Dive deep.

How do we distinguish the desires of the ego from those of the soul? There is no simple answer to this question. Sometimes, only time can tell. But you can ask yourself: If I don't satisfy this desire, will I regret it when my time comes to die? Will I look back and wish that I had followed my yearning? If the answer is yes, then you're probably dealing with a soul desire.

Our first response to the question "What do I want?" is often a confusing medley of thoughts and images. But then, as we continue to look inside, our true desires begin to surface, sometimes shyly, sometimes with explosive force, as if they had only been waiting for this opportunity to reveal themselves.

Defining what you want—in relationships, at work, or in family life—is the simple yet powerful gateway to fulfillment. "What do I want?" is not a question you ask yourself just once. It's like a mantra, an ever-present gateway to deepening insight and self-discovery. Naming your desires is the first step to fulfilling them. Every morning, ask yourself before you begin your day, "What do I want from this day?" If you define what you want, you're likely to have a more satisfying and fulfilling day.

tensity of our longing. Praying, in this sense, means letting yourself feel and *embody* your desire. It means revealing your desire without a trace of shame, so that your longing becomes an offering placed on the altar of life.

Asking for what you want is the litmus test that helps you discriminate between the more superficial desires of the ego and the deeper desires of the soul. If you can't ask for something from the bottom of your heart, it probably isn't a soul desire. Some desires are merely signs of a passing infatuation. Many desires we consider ours actually belong to other people. Ask yourself whether a desire is truly your own, or whether you are trying to fulfill the dreams of your parents, your partner, or society at large.

Sometimes, even though you sincerely believe you should pray for something, you may find that your soul refuses to cooperate. The words ring hollow and lack conviction.

This happened once to the 20th-century Indian teacher Vivekananda. When he was 21 years old, his father died, leaving the family of seven penniless and hungry. In vain, Vivekananda (whose name at that time was still Narendra) tried to find a job. Finally, he turned to his spiritual master, Ramakrishna, for help, well aware of Ramakrishna's miraculous powers. "Please pray to the divine Mother and ask her to remove my family's poverty," he pleaded. Ramakrishna refused. "You yourself must pray on their behalf," he said, and sent Narendra to the Mother's temple.

Narendra went to the temple determined to pray for financial help, but the instant he stepped over the threshold, the living presence of the goddess engulfed him like an avalanche, and he was overcome with ecstasy. Throwing himself at the feet of the deity, he stammered words of praise, all memory of his original purpose completely erased. Three times Ramakrishna sent Narendra back to the temple, and each time Narendra entered the temple determined to pray for money, only to have all his intentions washed away in a flood of ecstatic joy. In the end, Ramakrishna relented and blessed Narendra's family, who, thanks to the power of Ramakrishna's blessing, thenceforth never lacked the basic necessities of life.

This is not to say that we shouldn't pray for money. It doesn't matter what you pray for, so long as you pray from the depths of your soul. Many people are under the misconception that they

Dig beneath the superficial wants to find the deepest desire and ask how to satisfy that desire.

should not pray for material objects, only for spiritual gifts. This would be sound advice if the material world were spiritually insignificant, as patriarchal religion has often claimed. But if you assume that the soul has a purpose to fulfill in the world, which requires certain material necessities, it makes sense to pray that your deepest desires be granted, materially as well as emotionally and spiritually. In fact, when we fail to ask for what we need, we betray the holy presence within, which needs our full support in order to realize its goals in life.

In response to a student's question about what to pray for, Mother Meera, a contemporary spiritual teacher, answered, "Ask for everything—like a child asks its mother for everything without shame. Do not stop at peace of mind or purity of heart or surrender. Demand everything. Don't be satisfied with anything less than everything."[9]

Prayer works. This truth has been demonstrated again and again. For example, scientific studies have repeatedly shown that heart patients recover faster and have fewer setbacks if someone prays for them.

To be effective, however, prayer should grow out of faith and gratitude. When your prayer reflects an inner sense of lack, fear, or scarcity, it will not have much power. It's as if you were saying, "I want this but I don't believe I'm ever going to get it." In effect, you are proclaiming your lack of faith even as you pray. Not surprisingly, this doesn't work very well. Effective prayer is giving gratitude for something that has not yet happened.

In this arena, visualization can be of great help. Visualization teaches us to imagine that we already have what we want. It's not just a matter of seeing inner pictures, which some people find quite difficult. Rather, we use all our senses to imagine what fulfillment would look, smell, sound, taste, and feel like, making the experience as present and real as possible. In doing this, we take ourselves out of scarcity consciousness—the belief that there isn't enough to go around—and into a felt experience of abundance and fulfillment. The fact that this occurs only in imagination is irrelevant. Dreams, too, are imaginary, but if you have ever awakened from a nightmare trembling and sweat-drenched, you know the power of imagination. When we combine visualization and prayer, we own our desires and open to the visceral experience of their fulfillment.

The basic principle of visualization is very simple. Find an image of what you desire and dwell on that image until you feel the inner sense of satisfaction you crave. For example, a client of mine who wanted greater inner peace spent 5 minutes every morning entering into the following three images.

⚭ I'm having breakfast. I'm sipping a cup of my favorite tea and stroking my cat, which has curled up on my lap. I feel focused, refreshed, and centered. I'm looking forward to the day with calm and confidence.
⚭ I'm at work. I'm busy and challenged in all the usual ways, but I'm operating from an inner core of strength and radiant calm. People are attracted to my peaceful presence, and I enjoy my work more than ever before.
⚭ I'm in meditation. My room is simple and uncluttered, all white, with a bunch of yellow daffodils. Everything is quiet except for the sound of rain on the roof. I see myself sinking

deeper and deeper into a state of total love. I'm at peace with myself, at peace with my life, at peace with God.

Initially, visualization merely mimics the effects of true faith by evoking the feelings and sensations of gratification. Yet, provided that our prayers reflect the deep yearnings of our souls, they will be answered, though not necessarily in the way we expect. Thus, visualization can help us to deepen our faith.

When Jesus prayed, he prayed with total faith and hence with total conviction that his desires would be fulfilled. "If you have faith, everything you ask for in prayer you will receive," he said (Matt. 21:22).[10] In his case, there was no gap between desire and fulfillment. The two arose simultaneously, as when God said, "Let there be light"—and there *was* light. If your will is aligned with God's will, and if you have total faith, prayer is a surefire thing.

Cultivating Receptivity

In a famous story, a man comes to a Zen master seeking instruction. The master pours his new student a cup of tea, and then keeps pouring tea into the already full cup. When the startled student protests that his cup is overflowing, the Zen master points to the student's head and says, "What can I teach you? Your mind is like that cup—no space inside! First, you must make space. Empty your mind."

To receive, you must be receptive. This may seem obvious, but often we pound on life's door, demanding this and that, even though we aren't receptive. Our minds are crammed with ideas and preconceptions about how things are, how they should be, what's possible and what isn't. Many people aren't even sure what receptivity feels like. When they first experience it, they marvel at having missed out on such a delicious, rejuvenating state.

TRY THIS...

To experience receptivity, try meditating on the following images.

- God is liquid light and you are a dry sponge soaking up that light.
- You are an open bowl sitting in the rainshower of God's love.
- You are a flower standing in a field, opening into the light of the holy presence.
- You are a boulder, heavy, strong, and ancient, sitting on the earth, open to the sky.
- You are a cat basking in the sunshine. Every cell in your body is comfortable, relaxed, and open.
- You are an embryo and the universe is a safe, nurturing womb.

Lorna's Story

One of my clients was a woman in her forties who was severely disabled by a degenerative disease. Lorna had never had a truly satisfying sexual relationship and longed for one. But given her physical condition and her limited social life, where could she possibly find a suitable partner?

For many months, we talked about faith, receptivity, and the courage required to ask Spirit for what we want. Despite her pain and her doubts, Lorna began to embrace her desires. Then, one day she decided to respond to an ad in the personals section of her local

newspaper, placed by a man who said he was seeking a partner for sacred sexual encounters. Although I encouraged her, I also worried
that she might get rejected because of her physical condition.

Finding a partner through the paper is a risky business at best, and
in Lorna's case it seemed highly unlikely. Therefore, both Lorna and
I were amazed at what happened next. Lorna called the man, and he
sounded interesting enough that she decided she wanted to meet
him. I suggested that she tell him about her disability over the phone
before they met, and she did. "Oh, that's no problem," he replied
cheerfully, "I was married to a severely disabled woman for many
years." To make a long story short, Lorna and Jeff ended up falling
madly in love and having extraordinarily passionate, ecstatic sexual
encounters. Once again, I was reminded that miracles can and do
happen if we are open to them. Our skeptical, nay-saying minds do
not understand the ways of Spirit, and we had best tell our critical
judgment gently but firmly to stay out of the way when we pray.

If You Receive, You Will Have to Bear

Earlier in this chapter, I quoted Mother Meera's invitation to pray
for what we want. "If you ask, you will receive," she says. Then, she
adds cryptically, "If you receive, you will have to bear."[11]

I often recalled Mother Meera's words when I was around my
friend Joan, whose story I tell in my book *Aphrodite's Daughters*.
Joan was close to 40 years old when she met the man of her dreams.
The two fell in love, married, and looked forward to having a child
together. Then, just 9 months into their marriage, Tom was diag-
nosed with a fast-moving cancer, and 3 months later, he was dead.
Joan was wracked with unbearable grief and came close to losing
her mind.

One might think this experience would have caused her to turn
bitter and angry. But no. Today, Joan says that she would not undo

what happened for all the riches in the world. True to Mother Meera's precept, Joan asked for what she wanted, received it, and bore the consequences. Monastics may prefer the fires of renunciation to the burning heat of passion, but lovers have a different perspective. Far from regretting her prayers, Joan believes that in the midst of her pain and anguish, she received the greatest spiritual initiation of her life: "To love that deeply, to lose what I loved, and to discover the steadiness and strength that followed were much more transformative than 30 years spent meditating on detachment. I was attached, I suffered the loss, and I worked through it."

The Buddha was right—we do get attached to certain objects and people, and we suffer when we lose them. We cry when our pets die or when our lovers leave. But since when have valuable teachings not come at a price?

As Joan's story demonstrates, the fulfillment of desire brings its own set of often unanticipated teachings. Therefore we had better consider carefully what we pray for, and we must also understand that when we pray for something, we commit ourselves to a path without knowing exactly where it will lead. We are inviting desire to become our teacher and our guide, trusting it to serve as an angel of the highest powers.

Need Does Not Equal Weakness

If we are strongly invested in maintaining control, we will fear desire, especially sexual desire. Not only is sexuality notoriously difficult to control, but it crashes through any illusions we might harbor of being self-sufficient, independent individuals. More than any other form of desire, our sexual hunger forces us to confront the fact that we need each other.

We idealize independence and self-sufficiency. Yet in reality, every detail of our lives, from the clothing we wear to the food we eat, reflects the countless visible and invisible ways we depend on one another. Just consider the dozens, if not hundreds, of people involved in creating something as simple as the book you now hold in your hands.

Buddhism describes us as interdependent. Nowhere is our interdependence more apparent than in our sexual need for one another. Sexuality ties people together and drives them to reach out to each other. You can hardly convince yourself that you are a self-sufficient, independent being when every cell in your body is crying out for the touch of a lover. And you can't get out of bed after a night of passionate lovemaking and still believe that you are in control of the world, when obviously you're not even in control of your own body. If we buy into the belief that need equals weakness, we will feel ambivalent about our sexual desires. We'll perceive sex, with its sweet invitation to ecstasy, as a minefield.

We can succeed in deluding ourselves about our interdependence until it comes to making babies. At that point, nature lays down the law and reminds us that men and women each possess only half of the Creator's blessing: "On your own, you are incomplete. On your own, you cannot create new life."

Most societies accept interdependence as a given. We, however, are children of the era of control, which has idealized the value of independence, especially sexual independence. Sexual need has always been a thorn in the side of those who wished to transcend the world. There was only one solution to this dilemma—celibacy.

The problem with celibacy is that if everyone practiced it, the human race would die out. Nonetheless, many revered early Christian church fathers, such as Tertullian and Ambrose, were convinced that "if the only way to keep the human species alive was to have men and women endure the low and disgusting feelings and actions of intercourse, it would be better that the human race die out."[12]

Those early church fathers would have done well to consider the wise words of the 14th-century Japanese hermit Yoshida Kenko, who wrote that although sexual desire can make fools of us, it also possesses a mysterious power that merits the highest respect.

Sexual desire is an impulse which leads men into ridiculous situations. Here the nature of man is certainly folly. Strange to think what agonies men have suffered from a passion for some woman, and how a woman may lie tossing all night careless of all else and enduring inconceivable miseries from this passion. Such is the power of love.

But the truth is that it is rooted in deep things much beyond our knowledge and its source is far away indeed. There are desires attached to all the six senses, yet all but this one may be conquered. And from this neither the old nor the young, neither the wise nor the foolish are exempt.[13]

Coyote Pursues His Desire

Most indigenous cultures celebrate the power of desire as a life-giving, creative force. Native American mythology includes the wonderful figure of Coyote, the trickster god and hero of numerous rowdy and sometimes obscene stories. Coyote is desire incarnate. He's always hungry—for food, for money, and for sex—especially for sex.

More often than not, his plans backfire and the joke is on him. In a typical Coyote story, Coyote prepares to go to the dance with his friend Cottontail Rabbit.

Then it was night and they heard singing and dancing all about. So they went toward the music until Coyote said to Cottontail, "Stop a minute! You had better stay here. Women are very careful and suspicious of me," he said. "If I have this penis on, they are afraid of me. So you keep it for me here. When the women think I am all right, I will whistle. When you hear the whistle, bring my penis along."[14]

Just as he hoped he would, Coyote meets some lovely women, but by the time he's ready to whip out his penis, Cottontail is nowhere in sight—he is, in fact, busily using Coyote's penis in his own erotic exploits. As you can imagine, Coyote ends up in quite an embarrassing mess.

Yet we know that tomorrow Coyote will set out once again, undaunted and ready to embrace the world, as foolish-wise and as hungry for ecstasy as ever. Coyote, you must remember, is a god—a great and powerful god. In him we recognize the dance of the great hunger embodied. He teaches us to laugh at ourselves and at all the foolish tangles into which desire leads us, but he also invites us to honor the profound wisdom of desire.

CHAPTER THREE

Banishing the Demon of Shame

A key sign of healing is that your shame becomes less. . . . Shame exists in an environment of secrecy. When you begin to freely speak the truth about your life, your sense of shame will diminish.

—Ellen Bass and Laura Davis

One of the greatest ecstatics of all time was Mirabai, a 16th-century saint whose songs of yearning for God are still sung throughout India. Her own family, however, rejected her and even tried to have her murdered because she refused to behave like a traditional Hindu wife, and instead openly celebrated her love for the god Krishna. When people accused her of being shameless, she happily agreed: "Night and day, I cry for my Beloved, casting worldly shame and family custom to the winds."[1] Shedding shame—whether sexual, emotional, or spiritual—is a crucial step on the ecstatic's journey.

Ecstasy has no greater enemy than shame. To feel ecstasy is to say yes to life with every cell of your being. How can you say yes when shame is stubbornly saying no? How can you open fully to the source of love when you are poisoned with self-hatred? If we want to follow a path of ecstasy, we must purge ourselves of shame.

Shame has given us so many false messages about ecstasy that it may be helpful to remind ourselves of what ecstasy is *not*.

- Ecstasy is not frivolous.
- Ecstasy is not a dispensable luxury.
- Ecstasy is not a state of temporary insanity.
- Ecstasy is not meant to be a rare, once-in-a-lifetime experience.
- Ecstasy is not a threat to society.
- Ecstasy is not selfish. On the contrary, wanting it is a sign of health.

The Nature of Shame

Shame is different from guilt. Guilt tells us that we have done something wrong, something we should not have done. Shame, by contrast, tells us that we are fundamentally flawed, no matter what we do and despite all evidence to the contrary. Shame discounts our good deeds and interprets any mistake as proof of our basic, unalterable unworthiness.

Shame ambushes us at the slightest sign of weakness, pointing an ugly finger and yelling in a shrill voice, "See! Didn't I tell you so? You're just not good enough." And since its standards are superhuman—or, you might say, inhumane—shame never lacks for fodder. No matter how hard we try, perfection remains out of reach. So where does this leave us? Feeling as though we were born under a curse—which, according to the Catholic dogma of original sin, we were. We feel flawed in our very essence, doomed to eternal deficiency.

Shame undermines our ability to give and receive love. It makes us feel so undeserving that we build emotional walls and hide behind them. Then, shame gleefully points out that nobody loves us—when, in fact, we ourselves have walled love out. Shame insidiously creates the very thing we fear most: separation both from our fellow human beings and from Spirit. Under the relentless attack of shame, our sense of well-being crumbles.

To the extent that we believe the voice of shame, we are bound to feel afraid. If we are indeed unworthy, who will love us? Who will support us in times of need? Shame creates a constant and highly toxic undercurrent of anxiety in our lives that can undermine our health. When we fall ill, the bony specter of shame rises up all the more ferociously to tell us that we deserve no better, that we have made ourselves sick through bad living habits, that we have brought this upon ourselves. None of us lives immaculately, so who can disprove this claim?

The first time the Dalai Lama, the spiritual leader of the Tibetan community, visited the United States, he inquired about the sources of suffering in this country. Someone told him that one of our greatest problems was a general lack of self-esteem. The Dalai Lama looked puzzled. He didn't understand. Lack of self-esteem? What did those words mean? When he learned that many people felt flawed and unworthy, he shook his head in dismay. "This is very sad," he commented. He had never encountered this problem among his own people or in India, where he had lived since 1959. For his Western audience, it was an eye-opening moment that revealed how abnormal our epidemic of shame and low self-esteem really is.

Revisiting the Garden of Eden

Shame masks itself as a personal problem. In fact, as the Dalai Lama's reaction reveals, it is a culture-specific illness. If we want to understand the roots of our shame, we must examine not only our personal stories, but also the stories we collectively share. Among them, the story of Adam and Eve is especially illuminating because it specifically recounts the loss of ecstasy and the birth of shame.

As we all know, Adam and Eve lived in the garden of Eden, a place where joy drifted through the air like pollen, where every step was rapture and every breath brought bliss. They lost their beautiful home, however, after a snake seduced them into eating the fruits of a sacred, but forbidden, tree.

Many years ago, I had a dream that caused me to reexamine the meaning of this strange and fascinating story. At the time, I was quite out of touch with my body. I lived in my head, spent long hours hunched over books, and habitually tuned out undesirable physical sensations as though they were background noise. Then, one night, I had a dream:

I'm in a garden that has been neglected for a long time. The weeds reach my chest and some of the trees seem barely alive, strangled by climbing vines. Still, the garden hums with an intense, junglelike vitality. Cicadas chirp in the shadows and the full-throated song of blackbirds fills the air. There is a sense of magic and enchantment, but also of sadness and neglect.

As I pondered the dream, I understood that my unconscious had shown me an image of my own body—I myself was the negligent gardener, and my garden, though intrinsically healthy, was in disarray.

Intrigued, I turned to our civilization's oldest myth about a beautiful garden and found myself reading it in a new light. "The kingdom of heaven lies within," said Jesus. Now I realized that the garden of Eden, too, lies within. My dream was telling me, not that I had been banished from Eden, but that I myself had abandoned my inner Eden. I had neglected my inner garden for so long that I barely remembered its existence. Now it was inviting me to return.

The Tree and the Serpent

If Eden lies within us, then where is the sacred tree? And what about the serpent? They, too, lie within. When you look at anatomical charts of the central nervous system and the circulatory system, you'll notice how much they resemble a tree, with branches of nerves and blood vessels fanning out from the spinal column to bring life and consciousness to every part of the body. We even speak, aptly, of the "trunk" of the body. The story of Eden is one of many ancient myths that refer to this tree as the tree of life, also known as the tree of consciousness.

The presence of the life force in our bodies is what allows us to experience ecstasy.

Many myths also speak of a snake that glides, sinuous and silent, through the shimmering branches of the body-tree. Universally, the snake symbolizes the primordial creative energy of the cosmos in general and the life force within the body in particular. What we call ecstasy is the dance of the serpent through the tree of our consciousness.

In India, the serpent is called the *kundalini*, which means "the coiled one"—the full potency of God's embodied presence coiled at the base of each person's spine. The Kalahari Kung call the same force *num*, and they, too, describe it as an energy that lives at the base of the spine. The Kung awaken their *num* in all-night dancing and drumming ceremonies, and claim that doing this allows them to heal themselves and others.

If you think of your body as a house, the serpentine force is the electricity that flows through all the rooms and lights them up. Seen with the inner eye, every living body appears luminous—it shines, shimmers, and scintillates, each cell a little star. And ecstasy? Ecstasy is the joyful experience of the inner light.

The Vietnamese Buddhist teacher Thich Nhat Hanh wrote a book called *The Sun My Heart*. It was a title many people could immediately grasp. Though we may never have seen the inner light, most of us have, in moments of great love or joy, felt our hearts shining like a little sun—the body's own sun. But the heart is not the only part of the body that shines—it's just a place where we can most easily perceive the inner light. Wherever the life force is present, you can see luminescence—a subtle, fine-spun, and yet powerful radiance. Whether we call this energy *kundalini, num, chi, prana,* or the life force, its presence in our bodies is what allows us to experience ecstasy. Like liquid light streaming through our veins, the dancing serpent power engenders a flow of ecstasy and brings the soul tidings of God's presence. What we call ecstasy is the dance of the serpent through the tree of consciousness.

All spiritual traditions have developed techniques for triggering states of ecstasy by arousing the serpentine energy. Dancing, drumming, sex, the use of sacred plant medicines, yoga, and meditation all can awaken the inner serpent.

Cursing the Serpent

"When indigenous people talk about spirit, they are basically referring to the life force in everything," writes Sobonfu Some, a teacher from West Africa.[2] Most ancient cultures revered the life force and therefore revered snakes. Their myths portrayed the serpent not as an evil creature, but rather as a wise and sacred being. The Judeo-Christian tradition stands alone in its vehement condemnation of the serpent as an agent of evil.

The word *matter* is related to the Latin *mater,* the Mother. For tens of thousands of years before the arrival of the patriarchal Father God, people worshipped the Divine Mother in many different forms, all of them manifestations of nature, of the life force, and of the mysterious serpentine energy hidden within every atom of matter.

Then, a couple of millennia before Christ, a shift began that eventually led to the banishment of the ancient goddess and her replacement with a male god. The Bible is full of references to the need to eradicate her worship and kill her worshippers—testimony to the war that the followers of the new Father God declared upon the serpent-Mother Goddess.

For example, Jeremiah commands the Jews to give up their ancient religion. Yahweh himself, the prophet declares, is punishing them for the evil they have done in worshipping other gods. While the Jewish men listen in silence, the Jewish women, all staunch worshippers of the goddess, argue with Jeremiah: "We have no intention of listening to this word you have spoken to us in Yahweh's name, but intend to go on doing all we vowed to do: offering incense to the Queen of Heaven and pouring libations in her honor, as we used to do, we and our fathers, our kings and our leaders, in the towns of Judah and in the streets of Jerusalem" (Jer. 44:16–17).

Yahweh refers to goddess worshippers such as these when he commands his people to "tear down their altars, smash their standing stones, cut down their sacred poles. You shall bow down to no other god, for Yahweh's name is the Jealous One; he is a jealous God" (Exod. 34:13–14).

When we understand the historical context that gave rise to the biblical Eden story, we can appreciate it for what it is: the depiction of a showdown between two deities—one female, serpentine, and embodied; the other male, transcendent, and disembodied. The myth reflects the beliefs of a people who sided with the male deity and cursed the serpentine goddess.

No wonder Adam and Eve were confused. As children of nature, their instincts told them to obey the serpent, the ancient servant of the Great Mother, and to eat the apple she offered them. Yet in doing so, they drew upon themselves the wrath of the Father God. Suddenly, nature was no longer considered a trustworthy spiritual guide. Their instincts had betrayed them, it seemed. Pleasure was no longer good, and the path of goodness was no longer pleasurable. Ecstasy, so long revered as a pathway to the Divine, had become suspect and has remained so ever since.

Sexual Shame

As a child, my friend Peter was sent to Sunday school, where he terrorized the nuns by incessantly asking questions for which they had no answers. One day he demanded: "Why did Adam and Eve start wearing fig leaves after they ate the apple?"

Though his question stumped the teacher, she tackled it bravely. "Well, Peter," she said mildly, "they knew God was coming to visit them. Don't you put on your pants when your Daddy comes home from work?"

"No, ma'am," said Peter cheerfully, "in the summer, we all don't wear a stitch inside the house."

The nun blushed and quickly changed the subject. Nonetheless, Peter's question was a good one. Why did Adam and Eve run for cover? And why did they feel that only their genitals required covering? The true answer—though not one the sister was free to give— was that even though all our other body parts might deny their allegiance to the serpentine life force, our genitals will always remain its loyal and faithful servants. Incorruptibly truthful, they express their pleasure and displeasure, oblivious to the conscious mind's objections and warnings. And so, to cover the genitals is to cover the evidence of having betrayed the Father God.

The penis has a wisdom of its own. Unlike the more secretive wisdom of the vagina, the penis makes its desires known in obvious ways, sometimes much to its owner's embarrassment. Men often joke about their penises having minds of their own. In fact, a man's penis is his most innocent body part—the one body part that his ego can never fully control, the one body part that always remains faithful to its animal nature and to the purity of the serpent. A man's penis reflects and expresses his hunger for ecstasy even when he himself denies it. Therefore, Saint Augustine called the genitals sinful and declared that they "are rightly called pudenda"—literally, parts to be ashamed of—"because they excite themselves just as they like, in opposition to the mind which is their master, as if they were their own masters."[3]

Sexual energy is creative energy. Yet deep down, many of us believe that there is something wrong with our sexual needs and desires, our instincts and impulses, our fantasies and lust, and our sexual bodies. When we reject our sexuality, we cut ourselves off from the source of our creativity. How can we know the holiness of our own being when we distrust our basic nature? Therefore, sexual shame and spiritual shame always come hand in hand, like twin bullies sauntering into the school yard.

In a sense, we can trace all our sexual and spiritual problems back to the point at which we severed god from goddess, Spirit from nature. We defined Spirit as masculine, nature as feminine, causing a rift between the sexes that we are only now beginning to heal.

Over the centuries, the Judeo-Christian religions repressed the ancient techniques humankind once possessed for awakening the ecstatic inner dance of the serpent. The tree of consciousness was declared off-limits to human beings, and a hierarchy of guilt was established in which God blamed man, man blamed woman, and woman blamed the serpent.

The Birth of Shame

By eating the apple, Adam and Eve demonstrated their allegiance to the serpent energy and revealed themselves as beings of lust and desire, instinct and will, bundles of creative, impulsive, intuitive, rebellious energy. If the Father God was good and the serpent-Mother Goddess was evil, clearly they were evil, too. This they understood, and they expressed their shame by covering the seat of the serpentine energy within their own bodies. The tragedy of the story is not that they were forced to leave the garden and work for a living, but that they henceforth felt unworthy—joyful self-confidence gave way to shame.

Underneath the veneer of civilization, we too remain serpentine beings, fields of pulsating creative energy. Like the snake, we are sparks of natural intelligence, awash with waves of hunger and desire and longing. We cannot allow the sacred serpent power to move us so long as we fear it. Whenever we feel that our serpentine bodies are cursed and offensive in the eyes of God, we fall prey to shame and banish ourselves from the garden of Eden.

When we reject our sexuality, we cut ourselves off from the source of our creativity.

Of course, we are good at hiding our insecurities and displaying fake confidence. Yet, of the thousands of people with whom I have worked, only a handful possessed truly strong, intact self-esteem. In our society, shame and low self-esteem have reached epidemic proportions, eating away at the foundation of our happiness. "The problem is my thighs," a teenage girl told me the other day, knotting her smooth brow into a frown. A college professor with numerous credentials, including a Ph.D., said with a wry laugh, "My dad always told me I was stupid, and deep down I still believe him."

One person blames her body, another his mind. Ultimately, however, these are just the hooks upon which we hang our shame. Our specific insecurities are merely symptoms of a deeper-seated shame that hides out in the depths of our psyche, as irrational as the mad hatter, as tenacious as a pit bull, and as difficult to pin down as an eel. If you dig deep enough, you'll find the conviction that it is not okay to be an embodied, serpentine creature.

On the face of it, this belief sounds preposterous. Why would we reject our basic nature? Yet we do. We have absorbed centuries of shame about the fact that we are embodied beings rather than disembodied spirits. We are ashamed of the raw, pulsing power that lives within us, and of our problematic bodies, which exude all kinds of embarrassing substances: urine, feces, mucus, semen, and menstrual blood.

TRY THIS...

Whenever you feel shame, ask yourself: What message is shame giving me? Then write it down. No matter what it says, the voice of shame is not interested in helping you, only in putting you down and *keeping you down*. "I'm here to protect you," it may insist. "Without me, you'll make a fool of yourself." Don't buy it! Shame is not your friend.

Now, look at what you wrote and ask the most enlightened, wise, loving part of yourself to articulate why you should not believe the message of shame. Ask the voice of love to speak to you, and write down what it says. Ask it to help you to see through the lies that shame tells you. These lies may seem compelling. You may have heard them so many times that you believe them—but that doesn't make them true.

The voice of love doesn't flatter you. It won't tell you that you look like Marilyn Monroe when you are actually 50 pounds overweight. No matter what your faults are, however, love will never tell you that you are anything but lovable and basically good.

And then there are the feelings, sensations, urges, needs, and instincts that every infant experiences. All of them are open to censure, contempt, belittlement, and ridicule, starting with the eager hunger for the nipple, the rage at being left alone when the child needs body warmth and the comforting murmur of soft voices, the grief as Spirit seems to hide itself and the child feels stranded in a terrifying world, alone and abandoned. Increasingly, the divine light is obscured, the initial blaze of love dimmed and darkened until only a dim memory remains, and even that buried deep in the child's psyche.

Shame targets our insecurities and tells us that if anyone were ever to really see us, really get to know us, that person would run away in disgust. Not only is shame a liar, it also always addresses the childlike part of the psyche that is gullible, innocent, and vulnerable. The inner child usually accepts at face value what it is told, never suspecting that shame is lying. Without a strong ally, the inner child doesn't stand a chance when shame attacks.

The ally it needs is love—not sentimental, mushy love, but intelligent, critical, keen-sighted love. Intelligent love can easily analyze the messages of shame and expose them as lies.

The way to strengthen the voice of love is simple: Develop the habit of listening to it. Your psyche is like a radio that receives many different stations. Some delight in putting you down, criticizing and ridiculing you; others offer compassionate, clear guidance. Whenever you find yourself listening to the voice of shame, know that you have the power to change the channel and tune into a different station, one that broadcasts the voice of love. Sometimes it might take a little fine-tuning before you find the love station, but I assure you it's there.

Body Shame

For women, body image is an everpresent source of obsessive shame. Among teenage girls, in particular, anorexia and bulimia have reached epidemic proportions. We can point angry fingers at the tall, skinny fashion models with their extravagant beauty, but let's face it: Once internalized, the beauty ideals of our culture are not easily erased.

But that doesn't mean we have to hate our bodies forever. Instead of waiting for the media to change, we need to change the way we relate to our own bodies. Stereotypically beautiful women are no happier than others, nor do they have better sex. We have nothing to gain by criticizing ourselves, and a great deal of joy to lose.

Your body knows the way to ecstasy, but it will not guide you there if you consistently scorn it. Your body will not reveal its secrets as long as you approach it with disdain or consider any part of it ugly, disgusting, dirty, dangerous, polluted, or bad.

For me, one of the most helpful practices in healing physical self-hatred has been to shift my focus from the outside (how I look) to the inside (how I feel). When I pay attention to how I feel, I eat healthier food, move in healthier ways, and take better care of myself—not because the so-called experts tell me to do so, but because I am listening to the true expert: my own body. Only half in jest, I once suggested to a client that about 80 percent of our focus should be on how we feel and 20 percent on how others perceive us. She frowned and said, "For me, it's definitely the other way round—almost all of my attention is on whether people like me and how I look in their eyes. I hardly ever notice how I actually feel."

In tribal societies, people are very concerned with their looks and go to great lengths to adorn themselves. They are not forced constantly to compare themselves to unobtainable ideals, however. Marjorie Shostak, an anthropologist who spent several years living with the African Kung tribe, describes the pride young Kung girls take in their bodies.

> One day I noticed a twelve-year-old girl, whose breasts had just started to develop, looking into the small mirror beside the driver's window of our Land Rover. She looked intently at her face, then, on tip-toe, examined her breasts and as much of her body as she could see, then went to her face again. She stepped back to see more, moved in again for a closer look. She was a lovely girl, although not outstanding in any way except by being in the full health and beauty of youth. She saw me watching. I teased in the

!Kung manner I had by then thoroughly learned, "So ugly! How is such a young girl already so ugly?" She laughed. I asked, "You don't agree?" She beamed, "No, not at all. I'm beautiful!" She continued to look at herself. I said, "Beautiful? Perhaps my eyes have become broken with age so that I can't see where it is?" She said, "Everywhere— my face, my body. There's no ugliness at all." These remarks were said easily, with a broad smile, but without arrogance. The pleasure she felt in her changing body was as evident as the absence of conflict about it.[4]

I feel sad when I think of all the young girls in our society whose bodies are so beautiful, yet who feel ugly, flawed, and ashamed. In one of my workshops that included women in their fifties, sixties, and even eighties, I invited the four "maidens" among us to sit in the center, facing the older women. For the next hour, each of the older women talked to the young ones, telling them what she wished someone had told her in her own youth. The strongest message was: "Don't waste time criticizing your body. It's as perfect as it's ever going to be, so enjoy it now. Make peace with your body as it is, and love yourself."

Nakedness

Nobody can love us intimately unless we allow that person to see us. Do we have the courage to get naked, not just physically, but in every way—mentally, emotionally, and spiritually? To let go of all the masks, the cloaks, the armor, the protective shields, the coverings? To expose ourselves fully? Throughout the ages, physical nakedness has always symbolized the more profound nakedness of the soul, and physical vulnerability has symbolized spiritual vulnerability.

We are, as Buddhists put it, sentient beings. "May all sentient beings be happy," they pray. "May all sentient beings be peaceful." To be sentient means to be sensual, sensitive, and aware.

No matter how tough we might appear, both physically and emotionally, there is a place deep within us where we receive the touch of life with absolute freshness and tenderness, where we still feel the stinging lash of rejection and the healing balm of affection as deeply as any child does. Babies, kittens, and puppies touch our hearts because they remind us of that quiveringly alive, terrifyingly vulnerable place. The Indian spiritual teacher and philosopher Jiddu Krishnamurti once said, "If you are not interested in being sensitive, you might as well be dead—and most people are. . . . Do you know what it means to be sensitive? It means, surely, to have a tender feeling for things . . . , just because you are awake to the extraordinary beauty of things."[5]

Sensitivity is a double-edged sword. It awakens us to the world's beauty, but it also heightens our already uncomfortable sense of vulnerability. Therefore, exposing oneself, whether physically or emotionally, requires great courage. As the author Deepak Chopra points out, love forces us to reveal ourselves in the most vulnerable and intimate ways: "True love is more dangerous than most people are willing to admit. It arouses the same discomfort as in dreams where you find yourself naked in a public place. . . . To love another person involves opening up your whole being."[6]

When the 14th-century Kashmiri ecstatic Lalla attained enlightenment, she flung off her clothes and began to dance. From then on, she walked naked through the countryside, as free and uninhibited as a child, her physical freedom signaling the more profound freedom of her soul as she rejoiced in the divine presence. In one of her ecstatic songs, she celebrated her nakedness.

> *Dance, Lalla, with nothing on*
> *but air. Sing, Lalla,*
> *wearing the sky.*
> *Look at this glowing day! What clothes*
> *could be so beautiful, or*
> *more sacred?*[7]

Our culture teaches us to equate nudity with sex. Most situations in which an American adult is likely to experience nudity are sexually charged—during lovemaking, in advertising, or in sexually explicit films. Lalla's nakedness was not a sexual invitation, however, but an ecstatic expression of honesty, vulnerability, intimacy, self-acceptance, and sheer love of life.

Although nudity is never an official element of my workshops, participants sometimes express a desire to disrobe. Young children constantly demand to be looked at and admired, until they learn that "showing off" is a bad thing. Our beautiful, soft, rounded bodies need to be looked at and admired. Visual attention is as important to the erotic self as tactile attention, but our society offers few opportunities to receive the tribute of an appreciative eye.

In ancient Greece, initiates into the Eleusinian mysteries were led through a ritual that culminated in a "showing" of divinity. What exactly they were shown we will never know because they were sworn to secrecy; researchers speculate, however, that it may have been an ear of wheat, symbol of the goddess Demeter. Under normal circumstances, an ear of wheat would be an ordinary, insignificant thing, such as a wanderer might pluck from a field and mindlessly discard after playing with it for a minute or two. Yet just as beauty lies in the eye of the beholder, so does divinity. Presumably, by the time the initiates of the Eleusinian mysteries gazed upon whatever mysterious object they were shown, they had entered into that exalted state of consciousness in which things appear to shine as if illuminated from within.

Something akin to the Eleusinian mysteries has occurred, at times, when women have disrobed in my workshops. In those moments, the naked body is no more an ordinary body than the chalice used in the mass is a regular cup, or the Black Stone in the Kaaba at Mecca—which is more sacred to Muslims than anything else in the world—is a regular stone. Because the witnessing participants are fully clothed, the woman's nudity is highlighted, but not in a sexual sense. Rather, her nude body appears as a revelation of divinity, as Spirit incarnate shining through the luminous, mysterious curves and shadows of the human body.

The first time a woman asked to disrobe in a circle, I was unprepared for the power of the experience. Anthea, a woman in her forties who as a child had been sexually and emotionally abused, had worked for many years to reclaim her sense of integrity. Now, she wanted to dance for us—naked—as an affirmation of her growing self-love.

The night of Anthea's dance, we decorated the room with candles and flowers and lit a blazing fire in the fireplace. Anthea entered wearing a scarf loosely draped around her hips, but she soon discarded it. A full-bodied, full-breasted woman, she stood quietly and closed her eyes. Then, the dance began to rise through her body like an awakening serpent, undulating lazily and sensuously while her hands formed a triangle, sacred ancient symbol of the feminine.

The first few minutes of Anthea's dance, I was delighted to see her courage and pride—signs of the progress she had made over our years of working together. But somewhere in the middle of the dance, my vision shifted. Suddenly, I was no longer a contemporary woman. My eyes became those of an ancestor who had lived ten, twenty, thirty thousand years ago. We were in a cave, witnessing the sacred rites of the Great Mother. This was not Anthea, a victim of sexual abuse. This was not a woman who suffered because our misogynist society told her that she was overweight. Her body was no longer merely a symbol of the Mother—she *was* the Mother, mysterious beyond all words, the awe-inspiring, primordial feminine being whose blessing created and sustained us.

Only rarely have the women who undressed in my workshops been conventional beauties. Some have been overweight, others have been middle-aged or have borne mastectomy scars. Yet I, along with other participants, have felt nothing but awe and reverence as I gazed upon these women's naked bodies. Together, we have sensed a palpable wave of joy and gratitude washing through the circle as though some deeply buried longing within us was finally being acknowledged and satisfied. In such moments, we beheld Spirit incarnate in our midst. And because we knew these women to be as ordinary and flawed and wounded as any of us, we could not avoid the realization that the same extraordinary presence that we perceived in them abided within each one of us.

Fear of Ecstasy

In 1997, the author Thomas Moore published a book titled *The Soul of Sex*. As he traveled around the country, he found, much to his dismay, that the people who had enthusiastically celebrated his previous books were hesitant to discuss this new one. In a later article, he commented on this "profound resistance to life, a resistance often inspired and sustained by religion."

> I suppose I should have known ahead of time that traveling across America speaking about sex I would run into trouble. It's not that people are generally prudish about sex specifically, but, in a broader sense, we are distrustful of the life that continues to course through us in spite of our efforts at stability and security. We would prefer that life were not quite so lively.[8]

I agree with Moore—the resistance he encountered goes beyond sexual prudery. We are afraid of the life force within ourselves and of what might happen if we set it free. We are afraid of the immense passion that lies dormant within us, and of the waves this passion might cause in our lives if we ever let it loose. We are afraid of finding out who we really are and what our essential nature is. No matter what religious beliefs we personally hold, we belong to a culture that has deep roots in Puritan values. Consciously or unconsciously, we suspect our basic nature of being, if not evil, at least suspect and untrustworthy.

Yet all the great spiritual teachings of the ages assure us that our nature is not evil or untrustworthy. What streams through us—through our thoughts, emotions, and bodies—is profoundly good. As the author and teacher Alan Watts put it, "The rift between God and nature would vanish if we knew how to experience nature, because what keeps them apart is not a difference of substance but a split in the mind."[9]

We are afraid of the life force within ourselves and of what might happen if we set it free.

Within each of us, an ecstatic waits to emerge. Yet often, we refuse to let this inner ecstatic out. The very idea seems vaguely embarrassing, as if ecstasy might cause us to rip off our business ties and suits and dance naked down Wall Street, causing a sudden plunge in the stock market. We stand in the way of our own fulfillment and push aside what we intuitively know is our deepest desire.

Many of us secretly fear that if we ever opened the door to passion, all moral restraints would fall away and we would wreck our lives. We would sleep with our neighbors' wives, strangle our mean bosses, get drunk, and act excessively in all ways. Our fear takes us to exactly the same place where medieval man's fantasies took him—a realm of bestial depravity and unfettered self-indulgence that threatens to undermine the foundations of civilized society.

Ecstasy is a sign of serpentine activity, and because we have learned to fear the serpent, we stuff it back down whenever it rears its head. Automatically, often without even noticing, we suppress its sensuous undulations and stifle our life force. We keep our body movements small and contained, as if afraid of taking up too much space in the world. We choke back words of truth as they rise in our throats. We long to dance but don't, afraid of making fools of ourselves. We don't tell those we love how we really feel about them. In a thousand ways, we keep slamming the door on ecstasy.

"Who is the person inside you who wants to emerge?" I asked Nina, a woman in her early thirties. Immediately, Nina saw herself dressed in a splendid gold and red kimono, standing on the side of a mountain with her arms outstretched and her head thrown back, leaning into the wind.

"It's as if I'm flying," she said, "yet my feet are firmly planted on the Earth."

"It sounds as though you're describing a state of ecstasy," I commented.

Nina thought about this for a moment. Then she asked, "What is ecstasy?"

"Ecstasy," I said, "is the experience of full surrender to the life force."

Nina smiled and nodded. "Yes, that's it."

Yet, as much as she longed to become that blazing figure of joyous abandon, she also feared and resisted it. For months, Nina dialogued with her passionate, sensuous self, eyeing her warily from a safe distance. Then, ever so slowly, she began to acknowledge that to honor her hunger for ecstasy meant inviting this gold-and-red-robed figure into her life. To Nina's great relief, she found that her ecstatic self was not at all interested in wrecking her life and was quite capable of respecting limits and boundaries.

Becoming Shameless

By and large our lives are very isolated, compared to those of people in most traditional societies. Shame both breeds isolation and thrives in it. The one sure way to cut through shame is to share our truth in the presence of loving, respectful, and attentive allies. It is hard to describe the relief and amazement people feel when they realize how quickly a lifetime of shame can melt away in the presence of loving witnesses. Shame tells us to hide and to become invisible. Love invites us to come forward and be seen. By entering into sacred space together, we can create a field of love so powerful and so undeniably real that the fearful, shame-ridden parts of our being come out of hiding and reveal themselves.

In my workshops, people sometimes sing a little song to one another.

> *How could anyone ever tell you*
> *You were anything less than beautiful?*
> *How could anyone ever tell you*
> *You were less than whole?*
> *How could anyone fail to notice*
> *That your loving is a miracle?*
> *How deeply you're connected to my soul!*

It's a sentimental little ditty, but it never fails to pierce the veils of shame and remind us of our radiant, unsullied essence.

We are children of Spirit. As we begin to know this in a deeper way, love's roots take strong hold within the soil of our bodies and we become more and more shameless. By this I don't mean that we set out to offend other people's sense of propriety or to deliberately shock them, but that we become inwardly free. We know our own basic goodness in a visceral way and can afford to look realistically at our failings without succumbing to despair or self-hatred.

Spiritual love, like romantic love, is revolutionary and radical. Drunk with love, we no longer care what people think or whether they approve of us. When we feel the serpent power moving through our bodies, we welcome it joyfully, without apologies. When Spirit calls, we respond, like children who leap trustingly off a wall into their mothers' arms.

There comes a time in each of our lives when the inner serpent demands its freedom. We know that this time has come when we begin to long for new avenues of self-expression. We begin to dream of dancing with wild abandon, of writing poetry, traveling to faraway places, or making love with total freedom. Though we might be frightened, we yearn to take risks—to speak the truth when doing so feels risky, to reveal ourselves in new ways, to experiment, to explore the outer boundaries of our potential. Unlocking the cage takes courage, no doubt, but once we taste the joy of full self-expression, there is no turning back.

CHAPTER FOUR

Longing for Paradise

The place I found myself in was like a piece of heaven that had fallen to earth—so pure and pristine, as if man had never stepped foot on it. Flowers upon flowers as far as the eye could see, in all shapes and colors, framed in a green as radiant as life itself, with streams running here and there among sleepy groves—dream-like mirrors in which all this beauty repeated itself.

Hyacinths embraced tulips, jasmine blossoms entwined with rose petals, and the Judas tree scattered its scarlet bounty across the meadow. Here, even grains of sand looked like gold dust, and stones had the sheen of jewels. In the ponds fish darted like silver coins. Behind them rose an emerald green mountain overgrown with cypresses, poplars and teak trees, and from there, the breeze carried the scent of aloe and sandalwood.

—Nizami

Deep within, we all have a vision of paradise. Some people think it's a place where we lived long ago, in a golden age, before evil entered the world, before suffering, corruption, decay, and loss became humankind's constant companions. Others believe that paradise is where unborn souls live or where the virtuous dead reap the rewards of their righteousness. The Muslim's paradise is filled with poetry and dancing girls, the Christian's with harp music and angels. No matter how we envision it, paradise is a place we visit rarely and long for frequently. It's a place where colors glow with an otherworldly intensity, a place filled with roses and sweet-scented lilacs, flowing with milk and honey, a place where our loved ones never leave or die and where love never wavers or cools. It's a place that knows no harshness, where the world approaches us with exquisite gentleness, beauty, and love.

Ecstasy is the echo of paradise. Hearing that echo, the ecstatic is determined to re-create paradise on Earth. "It is possible," she insists, and her soul wants nothing more. Given the harsh and often cruel nature of the world, however, ecstatics inevitably meet with frustration and disappointment. The moments of ecstasy are, after all, so rare and so unpredictable, and the Earth seems so infinitely removed from the paradise of which they dream. The disparity between the inner vision and the outer reality is too great. Therefore, mystical poetry is often suffused with the musk of unsatisfied longing and the bitter aroma of brokenheartedness.

Honoring the Ecstatic's Grief

Perhaps the most powerful image of the ecstatic's grief comes to us from Haiti. There, the goddess of love is called Erzulie. Like Aphrodite, Erzulie is a lover of flowers and perfume, beauty and luxury, celebration and laughter, men and love itself. Erzulie's role is to bring a piece of paradise down to Earth, and for this reason she is particularly loved by the Haitian people, whose difficult and demanding lives afford them little access to the luxuries with which she surrounds herself. In her presence, everything sparkles with fresh dew and every moment is new, miraculous, and full of wonder. Pleasure, beauty, and harmony accompany her every move. The squalid world is transfigured and becomes a paradise where laughter ripples through the trees.

But every now and then, Erzulie falls into a terrible depression, an abyss of despair. In this state, nothing and no one can please or console her. In her study of Haitian religion, *Divine Horsemen*, Maya Deren describes how a person (it could be either a man or a woman) behaves when possessed by the goddess Erzulie Ge-Rouge.

> In the midst of the gaiety she will inexplicably recall, as women sometimes do, some old, minor disappointment. She will remark the one inadequate detail here among the dozen major achievements. Suddenly it is apparent that imperceptibly she has crossed an invisible threshold where even the most willing reason and the most ready reality cannot follow; and, in another moment, she, who seemed so very close, so real, so warm, is suddenly of another world, beyond this reality, this reason. It is as if below the gaiety a pool had been lying, silently swelling, since the very first moment; and now its dark despair surfaces and engulfs her beyond succor.
>
> Inevitably then—and this is a classic stage of Erzulie's possession—she begins to weep. Tenderly they would comfort her, bringing forward still another cake, another jewel, pledging still another promise. But it would seem that nothing in this world would ever, *could ever*, answer those tears. It is because of these tears that the women, who might otherwise resent her, are so gentle. In their real, reasonable world there is no grief like this.
>
> There are times when this sense of all things gone wrong is projected in that combined rage and despair which is Erzulie Ge-Rouge. With her knees drawn up, the fists clenched, the jaw rigid and the tears streaming from her tight-shut eyes, she is the cosmic tantrum—the tantrum not of a spoiled child, but of some cosmic innocence which cannot understand—and will not under-

stand—why accident should ever befall what is cherished, or why death should ever come to the beloved. . . .

So, Maitresse Erzulie, weeping, comes to that moment which has been called her paralysis. Just as the hurt of a child mounts and transcends both its own cause and solution, reaching a plateau where it exists as a pure pain, so her articulate complaints cease, even the sobbing; and the body, as if no longer able to endure, abandons the heart to its own infinite grief. . . . So she is carried from the stilled, saddened public to some adjacent private chamber. Stretched on the bed, her arms still outflung, she falls asleep as a child might, exhausted by too great a grief.[1]

Were Erzulie an actual woman, rather than a goddess, her lovers would certainly object that she is being unreasonable in her demands and is overreacting. A Western psychiatrist, confronted with a patient manifesting such behavior, might diagnose Erzulie as a bipolar manic depressive and medicate her.

But Erzulie is a goddess, which means that her personal idiosyncrasies are expressions of archetypal psychic configurations. To dismiss Erzulie as a manic depressive would be as foolish as to dismiss Jesus as a masochist. The ceremonies that lead to trance possession are the Haitian equivalent of what the mass is to a Catholic; through such rituals, the deepest patterns that inform our own journey are revealed to us.

Myths are important because they help us understand who we are and how we can relate to ourselves in a more skillful, compassionate manner. What Erzulie's myth tells us is that at times, we too will feel such inconsolable grief, and that this grief is not a neurotic glitch, not a pathological problem requiring years of psychotherapy or medication. Rather, our grief needs to be honored and acknowledged with reverence, as the people of Haiti acknowledge Erzulie's grief.

In fact, any spiritual seeker will understand Erzulie's pain. The fact that her rich and passionate love life ultimately fails to fulfill her tells us something about the nature of human loves, which never turn out quite as ecstatic or as perfect as our imagination might picture them, and which inevitably contain the seeds of disappointment.

Life, one of my teachers used to say, is like the curly tail of a dog. We can try to straighten it out, but it's going to curl back up on us. Like that dog's tail, our lives will always have their kinks; they will never look quite the way we think they should. We can't help trying to improve things, and we can't help failing. From God's vantage point, all may be well with the world, but from ours, it isn't. Every day, we witness things that are most definitely *not* all right by us. Faced with the realities of warfare and starvation, injustice and cruelty, grief is an entirely natural and appropriate response.

The chalice Erzulie holds up in communion is filled with the tears of her despair for the world. Erzulie, who is herself the embodiment of paradise, of all loveliness and enchantment, realizes that her golden light can never grace the whole of creation, and that just beyond the pale of her sphere, ugliness and mean-spiritedness will raise their ugly heads. And because she herself is paradise embodied, she cannot abandon her ideals and pretend that all is well.

Her tears reflect the pain of our own yearning for the exquisite, light-bathed perfection of the spiritual world that can never be achieved within the physical dimension, or, if achieved for a moment, cannot be maintained. Her despair provides the counterpoint to the extraordinary sense of celebration she brings to every gathering. Erzulie *must* grieve, because there is no way to bridge the chasm between the harsh realities of earthly life and the transcendent, unearthly beauty she herself embodies.

Such suffering, her myth informs us, is not a sickness or a sign of dysfunction. Rather, Erzulie teaches us to open our hearts with compassion, not only to others, but to ourselves in our grief and our outrage, and to honor the emptiness, pain, and anger we all feel in the face of disappointment and betrayal.

Ecstasy and Suffering

Erzulie is a beautiful yet turbulent goddess, a goddess given to extremes of both ecstasy and suffering. We normally expect gods and goddesses to have more power and control than we do. But Erzulie has remarkably little control. She can't lessen the terrible intensity of her grief, she can't shorten its duration, and she can't determine when she will descend into depression or when she will return to her usual state of joyful celebration.

Yet, in her very lack of control Erzulie communicates a powerful message: Ecstasy is always a gift of grace. Its comings and goings cannot be controlled—not even by the goddess of ecstasy herself. If we would honor our hunger for ecstasy, we must also acknowledge our lack of control. There is much we can do to entice the spirit of ecstasy, but ecstasy has the wild soul of a gypsy—today it may abandon the place where it camped yesterday. Today's source of pleasure may ring hollow tomorrow. Or, as Rumi puts it, "God's joy moves from unmarked box to unmarked box."[2]

Like Erzulie, many ecstatics feel as though they are riding the wildly undulating back of a huge snake. One moment, they touch the heavens, the next, they are writhing in hell. In mystical literature, songs of desperate lamentation stand side by side with songs of exultation and jubilant praise. In one poem, the 16th-century Indian poet Mirabai declares that, having made love to Krishna, she is the luckiest woman alive. In the next, she's wailing in despair.

Our love affair with life must be founded not on infatuation but on a clear-sighted awareness of what the spiritual journey really requires of us. Certain New Age teachings would have us believe that if we play our cards just right, we can rid ourselves of suffering. We need never get sick or old, we need never be struck by disaster, we can live in a state of constant joy and delight. Unfortunately, this is nothing but wishful thinking. If you study the lives of God's lovers, you'll find that most of them suffered deeply.

God loves you, parents tell their children. But how do we really know that God loves us? Surely not by how well things are going for us. Only childish minds assume that an easy life is proof of God's love, or that hardships are caused by God's anger. Unless we know the spirit of love in the midst of suffering and loss, we don't know it at all.

If we acknowledge how deeply we long for ecstasy, we also have to acknowledge that we suffer in its absence. It should not surprise us to discover that in her grief, Erzulie adopts the posture of crucifixion, with arms outflung and head limp, and that her special symbols are the cross and the pierced heart. Deren describes Erzulie as "the dream impaled eternally upon the cosmic cross-roads where the world of men and the world of divinity meet."[3]

Like Erzulie, we too are impaled upon the crossroads between our divinity and our humanity. Erzulie's myth describes the cross that every ecstatic must bear, and shows us the necessity of embracing the inevitable suffering of this path.

Much as we might wish it were otherwise, the ways of ecstatic love are rarely straightforward. Spirit seduces us, drawing us from the straight and narrow path into ambiguity and uncertainty. Over and over, it crushes our illusion of having things under control and humbles us. Ecstasy appears suddenly, when we least expect it. Then, just as we settle into its delicious embrace, it vanishes like a chimera. Even after awakening to the truth of our eternal oneness with Spirit, we forget. Suddenly, we feel desperate and confused, abandoned in a bleak, hostile world.

In Hindu mythology, the ways of Krishna, the supreme lover, are always described as circuitous, devious, and sneaky. When he is portrayed in dance, the dancer will hold out two fingers like scissors, imitating the undulating movement of a snake gliding through the underbrush. Immediately, the audience knows to whom she is referring—God appearing in the guise of irresistible temptation, heart-stopping beauty, and infuriating inconstancy.

In Africa, it is believed that only evil spirits move in straight lines.

Everything wholesome curls and curves, undulates and turns, cycles and spirals. Death moves in a straight line, hatred and spite move in straight lines, propelled toward their targets like bullets. Love, on the other hand, is drawn to rounded limbs and curving lips. It circles gracefully like a dove, diving down to caress a cheek or a bare shoulder. Therefore, the path of love always curves and spirals—so much so that at times we seem to be regressing, rather than progressing, on our path.

The stories of ecstatics are full of surprising ups and downs, twists and turns, over which they have no control. Often, they freely acknowledge that they have no idea why their suffering turned to ecstasy when it did. In the following passage, the Eskimo shaman Aua, who lived in the first half of the 20th century, describes the roller-coaster journey of his initiation:

> I sought solitude and here I soon became very melancholy. I would sometimes fall to weeping, and feel unhappy without knowing why. Then, for no reason, all would suddenly be changed and I felt a great, inexplicable joy, a joy so powerful that I could not restrain it, but had to break into song, a mighty song, with only room for the one word: joy, joy! And I had to use the full strength of my voice. And then, in the midst of such a fit of mysterious and overwhelming delight, I became a shaman, not knowing myself how it came about. But I was a shaman. I could see and hear in a totally different way.[4]

Vanya's Story

My friend Vanya is, in many ways, the very embodiment of Erzulie—a great lover of celebration, of pleasure, of men, and of love itself, a tremendously passionate, vibrantly alive woman whose ecstasies are as high as her despair is deep.

TRY THIS . . .

Sit down with pen and paper in a quiet, private space. Close your eyes and spend a few minutes breathing deeply, calming yourself, and bringing your mind into the present moment.

We've all heard God referred to as the Creator. Right now, I invite you to consider that God is indeed a creator—an artist, in fact, the greatest artist of all time. Imagine, now, that each human life is one of God's paintings. In our eyes, some paintings seem more successful than others, but in God's eyes, they're all masterworks—breathtakingly beautiful bursts of vitality and energy.

Moreover, in God's eyes, every life is a self-portrait—a unique and perfect expression of an aspect of God's own being. Just as God is infinite, so are God's expressions. Each life is unique and perfect.

What kind of painting do you envision when you look at your own life? What colors do you see? Is your life a Rembrandt, with glimpses of light breaking through rich, dark browns and black? Or is it an Impressionist piece in soft greens and blues? Are the

Vanya had been no stranger to suffering, but when the most passionate and ecstatic relationship of her life ended, her whole world collapsed. She had glimpsed the possibility of a perfect love. "I had seen the gloriousness of us," she recalls. "I had known the highest ecstasy. I couldn't imagine feeling that alive, that creative, without his juice. I couldn't see myself as whole without him. In Tantra, they speak of the union of perfected opposites. We were that."

After breaking up with her lover, Vanya could not bear the overwhelming intensity of her grief—grief not just for the loss of her shapes clearly outlined, or does one flow into the next? Is it a delicate miniature or a wall-size mural?

Pick up your pen and paper and describe the work in progress that is your life. Try to see it as God might see it, with total love and appreciation. Notice that those moments you consider low points in your life are essential to the integrity of the whole painting. Without that black chasm, without that jagged line, without that sudden explosion of darkness in the lower left-hand corner, this painting would not be the masterpiece it is.

As you contemplate the painting of your life, write down what you see without imposing an interpretation. Notice the purple and the magenta without demanding to know what purple and magenta mean. This is an exercise in intuitive appreciation, not intellectual analysis. Breathe deeply, allowing your sense of appreciation to fill your body and warm your heart. With all its pleasures and pains and triumphs and disappointments, your life is just as it should be. Let your inner gaze be a blessing on this extraordinary miracle, your life.

lover, but also for the loss of the paradise they had shared. To numb her pain, she became an alcoholic.

> I drank myself into oblivion for 2 years, trying to self-destruct. Alcohol became my daily obsession. Every morning, I would wake up and think: "Okay, you have to make yourself happy." I thought I would die otherwise, the suffering was so intense. I couldn't face the loss. And I couldn't be around any of my friends.

I would work a split shift, hang out in the bar from 7:00 in the morning till about 2:00, go home and sleep it off, and go back and do the night shift till 2:00 A.M., then drive home drunk, go to bed, crash, and start all over again the next morning. I am ashamed to say that I drove drunk all the time. I must have had one heck of a guardian angel.

Many addicts are people who respond to life in intensely emotional ways but, unlike Erzulie, they have not learned to bear their crosses and to accept both ecstasy and suffering. Erzulie makes no attempt to avoid the inner darkness that descends on her, but stays fully engaged with her suffering. She never tries to distract herself, let alone numb or medicate herself with drugs or alcohol.

Like all fruits of nature, ecstasy ripens in its own time. The dark, lean seasons of our lives have a fresh, invigorating goodness of their own, like the crisp cold of winter. Addicts—and we all have addictive tendencies—find the rhythmic dance of union and separation intolerable. Because their yearning for the ecstatic state is so intense, they have little tolerance for deprivation. They would like to artificially shorten the wintery periods of separation or, better still, do away with them entirely, so as to live in a state of uninterrupted rapture. But ecstasy refuses to be forced in this way—the substance or activity that initially seemed a sure source of pleasure eventually sours and becomes a demonic presence in our lives.

Even in the midst of her alcoholism, however, Vanya never lost her willingness to say yes to Spirit and to her own healing. The instant the door to wholeness opened, she walked through and never once looked back.

Two things came together in Vanya's healing. First, she was blessed by an act of grace, much as Aua was. Her change of heart happened suddenly, without any effort on her part. Yet no amount of grace can save someone who is not willing to be saved. Vanya wholeheartedly embraced her rebirth. Touched by Spirit, she instantly let go of alcohol and threw herself into rebuilding her life with the same passionate intensity with which she had previously pursued her self-destruction.

> One morning, a miracle happened, a true miracle. I woke up broke, with a hangover, as usual. I remember looking out the window and it was a clear, beautiful day. The sky was bright blue with little clouds moving through. Somehow, I went into a deep sense of appreciation and gratitude. This feeling was pure grace. I never invited it. It just happened to me. It was an energy that descended into me. I appreciated what a beautiful room I had. I had five dollars in my pocket, and it felt like a million. I felt so grateful for that. I felt gratitude for the clouds. I remember thinking that I had plenty of friends, and that I would not starve. Then I took an inventory and found that I had a couple of cans of tuna fish, a little milk and bread, and some food for my cats. Suddenly, I felt such a sense of relief. I knew that I had hit bottom and that I would go no further down. And my heart started swelling. There was this immense, swelling knowledge that the universe was going to take care of me, and that I would be provided for. I stopped drinking that morning, and never thought about doing it again. I stayed home very quietly all day. It was the first night I didn't go to the bar. I took my five dollars, went to a movie, and loved every moment of it. Ironically, that movie was called *The Turning Point.*

We tend to think of suffering as the opposite of ecstasy. In fact, the opposite of ecstasy is not pain but *numbness*—the death-in-life that descends on us when we close down to life. It takes courage to lead an ecstatic life because the ecstatic chooses to be fully alive, open to the entire spectrum of life's experiences, including both rapture and agony. Feeling agony doesn't mean wallowing in it. The ecstatic does not seek out pain or build an identity around his suffering, yet he accepts it as part of the terrain he must cover on his journey.

As Vanya's story shows, you can't have the light and refuse to know the dark. If you do—if you refuse to feel the pain life hands you—you'll become an addict. Many of us in whom the hunger for ecstasy runs strong have at some point grappled with the dangerous lure of addiction. In the next chapter, we'll take a closer look at addiction and how it manipulates our longing for paradise.

CHAPTER FIVE

Grappling
with Addiction

*Many people in our society are being driven to addictions because there is
no collective container for their natural spiritual needs. Their natural
propensity for transcendent experience, for ritual, for connection to some
energy greater than their own, is being distorted into addictive behavior.*

—Marion Woodman

Addiction—whether to alcohol,
drugs, shopping, food, material consumption, sex, or anything else—
is the shadow side of the hunger for ecstasy. You may recall a story
from your childhood—*The Red Shoes*, by the 19th-century Danish
writer Hans Christian Andersen. Most storybook versions soften the
horrendous brutality and cruelty of the original tale. Nonetheless, it
is useful to revisit the original. It reflects values and beliefs about
desire, addiction, and the hunger for ecstasy that many of us internalized while we were growing up, and it can help us to get in touch
with important truths about ourselves and our relationship with
desire.

The heroine of the story is a little girl so poor that she has no
shoes save an old pair of wooden clogs. When winter comes, little
Karen's feet turn red with cold. Moved by pity, the shoemaker's wife
makes Karen a pair of shoes from leftover scraps of red felt. Soon after

this, Karen's mother dies, and the child sadly follows the coffin in her little red shoes.

Just then, a black carriage trimmed in gold and lined with velvet drives by. In it sits an old woman who notices Karen. When she hears of Karen's orphaned state, she announces that she will take Karen home with her.

"Oh," Karen thinks, "she just wants me for my pretty shoes." But no. The old woman thinks the red shoes are hideous, and she burns them along with Karen's other clothes. She gives the girl new clothes and teaches her to read, write, and sew.

But Karen grieves the loss of her red shoes. And so, when she spots a pair of brand new, bright red dancing shoes in the shoemaker's shop, no power on Earth can stop her from having them. Not only does she buy them, she wears them to church, which the villagers consider a blatant act of immodesty.

As Karen walks out of church that Sunday, she sees a man with red hair and a red beard lounging against the cemetery wall. "Nice dancing shoes, eh?" he chuckles, and Karen just can't help herself— she just has to twirl around and show off her pretty shoes. She twirls and twirls and twirls some more. To everyone's horror, she cannot stop dancing. Although she is by now exhausted, she keeps on dancing until the shoes are ripped from her feet and she is forbidden to wear them ever again.

We all know that when something is forbidden, it becomes all the more desirable. One day Karen sneaks into the room where the shoes are stored and puts them on.

This is the day the devil has been awaiting, for the red-bearded man lounging outside the church was he. As the poor girl walks through the woods in her red shoes, the devil waylays her and begins playing his fiddle. Once again, Karen starts dancing and cannot stop. This time, however, no one comes to her rescue, no one stops the mad frenzy. Faster and faster she dances, until she realizes that these shoes are to be her death.

Finally, as she dances past the hangman's house, she implores him, "Hangman, please cut off my shoes, for they are of the devil and will be the death of me." The hangman tries but cannot, for the cursed shoes will not leave her feet.

"Then, hangman," she weeps, "you must cut off my feet."

And so he does. Only then can the poor girl rest, while the shoes dance off into the world by themselves, leaving her a crippled beggar to the end of her days.

This is a strange bedtime story indeed, one more likely to give children nightmares than sweet dreams! And even the version I have recounted omits some of Andersen's most gruesome flourishes.

Here we have a girl who follows her desire and discovers, in her red shoes, a pathway to ecstasy. The shoes, however, are the work of the devil. They are specially designed to seduce and destroy her. The moral is clear: Beware of your desires because the devil will use them to sink a hook into your soul. What might seem like a harmless craving can turn into a powerful and uncontrollable obsession that will destroy your life overnight.

Spiritual Starvation

The story of the red shoes unfolds against a backdrop of poverty and deprivation. Such bleak and joyless realms are prime breeding grounds for crime and addiction. Wherever the hunger for ecstasy is denied, the soul becomes ravenous, and a ravenous soul has little access to wisdom. Karen's tragedy is not her stubborn insistence on having what she wants, but the villagers' failure to acknowledge her legitimate needs. They abandon her when she most needs help, and they feel so threatened by her red shoes and everything they stand for that they can only see them as the work of the devil.

The story obviously blames Karen's vanity for the tragedy that befalls her. A more compassionate view, however, would hold that she has been framed, so to speak, by being starved of love and pleasure to the point of desperation. Here we have a child who is blessed with an irrepressible hunger for ecstasy, yet finds herself orphaned and trapped in a society determined to repress that very hunger.

Outwardly, contemporary American society could hardly be more different from Karen's world of poverty and hunger. Yet, we suffer from our own brand of cultural and spiritual poverty. That most of us experience ecstasy rarely, if ever, is cause for alarm. Addiction is bound to remain an enormous social problem as long as people's hunger for spiritual communion goes unfed.

How many of us have put on the red shoes and then found, to our distress, that we could no longer take them off? The story of the red shoes reminds Linda, a 50-year-old professional, of her years as an alcoholic. Although Linda never knew hunger or want, she grew up in an emotional and spiritual wasteland, poorly mothered and poorly loved. Alcohol became her red shoes. What initially gave her pleasure later took over her life—the gateway to ecstasy became demonic. For years, Linda danced the dance of the alcoholic, unable to stop even though she could see that the dance was leading her to her death.

All energy, including life force, must move and flow. You cannot simply stash it away. So if your desire energy is strong, you had better figure out how to relate to it wisely. Without wisdom to guide you, desire energy can destroy you. It can make you eat your way to obesity, drink your way to ruin, and work your way to a heart attack. Many of us recognize ourselves in Karen's loneliness and in her passionate insistence on having those red shoes. We identify both with her desire and with the suffering she endures because of it.

Ruth, a heavyset woman in her sixties, is a recovering bulimic. When she heard the story of the red shoes, she immediately sympathized with Karen. Ruth saw in Karen a woman who dared to live fully, no matter the price. Hesitatingly, in a faltering voice, Ruth told me about her struggle with sexual desire. As a young woman, she began using the permissible pleasures of food as a substitute for the dangerous, forbidden pleasures of sex. She would eat until she went numb, then look at herself in the mirror and say, "Now you're so fat, nobody will want to have sex with you anyway."

Remembering this, Ruth looked down, her face drawn with pain. "I've never even dared to try on the red shoes. I've always been too scared. Is it too late now?"

I told her that as long as there's breath in our bodies, it is never too late to embrace our desires or to experience the rapture of being fully alive.

Addiction to Consumption

God, it seems, has planted an insatiable longing in our souls. Longing for what? For love? For joy? For beauty?

No, say the commercials. What you need is a new car, a sexy girlfriend, a trip to the Bahamas. What you need is a no-hassle lawnmower, a low-fat cereal, or a sure-to-flatten-your-abs workout video.

Runaway desire fuels the economy, and many of this country's most creative minds are dedicated to the art of arousing it. They awaken artificial needs in us, making us sick with desire. Then, like charlatans, they tell us to hand over our money so that they can cure us. "Life is short," they cry, "Hurry! Hurry! Supply is limited!"

Consumerism intentionally cultivates greed in the general public. And what is greed? It is misdirected desire—desire for something that will never satisfy the soul.

By exploiting the erotic for financial profit, with no trace of reverence for the sacred power of Eros, commercial society insults the ancient god in the worst possible way. In the end, the loss is ours as Eros turns away in disgust. Drained of all luminosity and sacredness, desire becomes shallow and meaningless and no longer serves as a raft to carry us to the realm of the sacred.

When we rush to satisfy our desire, whether for a new car or for an orgasm, we are, in effect, trying to escape the uncomfortable experience of desire itself. We do not want to feel it. We would like to get rid of it quickly, and we believe that buying the car or having the orgasm will accomplish just that. And so it does—for a while. But within no time, desire returns in a new form. If we relate to desire as something to get rid of by satisfying it as quickly as possible, we learn nothing from it. Instead of feeling that our desire is a problem or an illness that needs to be cured, can we feel grateful for its enlivening presence? Can we simply *be* with it, without grasping for premature satisfaction? This is the addict's greatest challenge.

Millions of people we might never think of as addicts are, in fact, driven by addiction. Take Sandy, an attractive woman in her thirties. Sandy is a shopping addict who owns not just one but several pairs of red shoes, all crafted of the finest Italian leather and purchased with one of her many credit cards.

> My mother never touched me and I was totally love-deprived as a child. All my senses were starving. I was ravenously hungry for praise, for attention, for beauty, for food, for touch, for color. When I grew up, I discovered shopping. Shopping was officially sanctioned. Women were *supposed* to shop. So I shopped. Mostly, I bought clothing. Nobody questions you when you buy a thousand dollars' worth of clothing. Nobody says, "Are you sure you can afford this?" They treat you like royalty, like you're the queen of England. It's not at all like being

a drunk, where everyone looks down on you. In fact, it's just the opposite—the more you spend, the better they treat you.

Female shopping addicts often believe that beauty is the key to love: If they are beautiful enough, perhaps someone will love them. But once they buy that new dress or that new pair of shoes, the purchase loses its glamour and they feel no more beautiful or loved than before.

I believe that the addiction to consumption is especially dangerous because we don't see the damage we're doing when we go shopping. So long as we can afford it, we see no harm in indulging ourselves. We don't have to acknowledge that our "harmless" fun may be doing irreversible damage to Earth's environment. We read about poisoned air and rivers, burned rain forests, and dying species, but they seem far removed from our lives and we don't feel personally responsible. We don't link those problems to the new appliances or the new cars we just purchased. Most addictions take their heaviest toll on the addicts and their immediate families. In this case, however, we're expecting future generations to pay the price for our reckless self-indulgence.

Searching for Diamonds

A traditional Sufi story tells how one night, the holy fool Nasruddin was found searching the road under a streetlight.

"What are you doing, Nasruddin?" his friends inquired.

Nasruddin sighed, "I lost a diamond."

"Where did you lose it?"

Nasruddin pointed toward the woods. "I took a nap under a tree, and it must have fallen out of my pocket."

His friends were puzzled. "Why are you looking for it here, when you lost it over there?" they asked.

TRY THIS . . .

List five material desires you have—objects you would like to buy or possess. They might be small ("I'd like to buy that silk scarf I saw yesterday") or extravagant ("I'd like to own a second home in Tuscany"). Don't censor any desire as unreasonable or too outrageous.

Now, look at each desire and ask yourself, "What would it feel like to satisfy this desire? What would the inner experience be?" For example, perhaps you imagine that buying that scarf would make you feel pampered, wealthy, or beautiful. Underneath each desire, write down the inner experience you crave. For example, "I want to feel beautiful. I want to feel pampered. I want to feel wealthy."

Now, close your eyes. Imagine having the inner experience that you crave. Imagine feeling—for example—beautiful, pampered, and wealthy. Breathe deeply and open your whole body to

Dazzling them with his happy, foolish smile, he said, "Well, the light is better here."

The diamond is a universal symbol of that spiritual essence within all of us that is eternal, precious, and stunningly beautiful. Like Nasruddin, the addict searches for his lost diamond in places where he'll never find it—in wine bottles, in lines of cocaine, or under the bright lights of shopping malls. But where did he lose his diamond? He lost it wherever he fell asleep to the divine presence, wherever ignorance and unconsciousness overtook him. To find it, he must leave the well-lit thoroughfares and head back into the shadowy woods of his own heart and soul.

the experience. Let the sense of well-being and satisfied desire spread like a delicious warmth to envelop your heart and nourish your belly. Take a few minutes to bask in this pleasure.

You are empowering yourself to have what you want right now. You don't have to wait to buy that scarf to feel beautiful. You don't have to spend a penny to feel wealthy. Every outer object you ever craved was desirable only because of the inner experience with which you associated it. You have the power to trigger that same experience just by using your mind and your imagination.

By intentionally evoking feelings of security, well-being, and abundance, you are claiming the power to shift your moods, enhance your self-esteem, and control your emotions. You may still decide to go out and buy that scarf. But you'll know that you don't need to have it in order to feel the way you want to feel.

Rewriting the Story

In an abusive or dysfunctional family, often there is one child who insists on having those "red shoes." Her family considers this one the black sheep, the one who just can't fit in. Like the villagers in the Andersen's tale, her siblings will find ways to adapt to the repression. They'll cling to unquestioned, narrow, cut-and-dried judgments. No red shoes in church, please.

But this child rebels against repression. Her hunger for ecstasy is too strong. In all likelihood, she will initially feel guilty and ashamed for being who she is. "I'm selfish and greedy," she thinks, sadly. She isn't supposed to have such strong needs and wants. She's supposed to be grateful for what she is given. Yet she can't get the red shoes out of her mind. Those red shoes are Spirit calling to her.

We need to discriminate clearly between superficial ego desires and the deeper hunger of the soul. Confusing the two leads to addiction, because we keep trying to satisfy deep spiritual needs with superficial substitutes that can never address the soul's hunger for ecstasy. The soul's needs are always aligned with health and growth; superficial ego desires, when they turn into addictions, become destructive. Addiction overrules the desire for health, sometimes even the desire for life itself. Recovery begins with the choice to reorganize one's priorities—to choose life over death, health over sickness, sobriety over intoxication, reality over illusion. Recovery requires us to get in touch with our desire to live, to thrive, to walk in balance. The first steps in disentangling ourselves from addiction lie not in deciding to deprive ourselves, but in examining what we really want and taking our deepest desires seriously. Recovery, in other words, requires us, not to renounce desire, but rather to get in touch with an even more potent, deeper desire. As the psychologist Carl Jung recognized, the need for alcoholic spirits is a distorted, literalized expression of the need for Spirit.

> *We need to discriminate clearly between ego desires and the hunger of the soul. Confusing them leads to addiction.*

Recovery from addiction is a spiritual path, as the various 12-step programs emphasize. We cannot simply will ourselves to desire health or sobriety. The desire for health is what I would call a desire of the soul, as opposed to the sometimes warped desires of the conditioned mind. No amount of willpower can connect us with the passionate desire of the soul—this requires an act of grace. Our prayer, then, should not be that God liberate us from desire, but that we be graced to know the desire of the soul.

What would Eros say to those among us who struggle with anorexia and bulimia, to those who shop compulsively, running up credit card bills they cannot afford, to those who are addicted to alcohol and drugs and sex? I believe that he would tell us that desire is not a spiritual hindrance. We need not chop it off, like Karen's dancing feet, in order to approach God. On the contrary, desire is an angelic messenger. If we honor our desires—*really* honor them—they will become gateways to wholeness.

CHAPTER SIX

The Ecstatic's Discipline

> *"What is the highest that man can achieve through practice?" I frequently asked Eastern masters. The reply was always, "The readiness to let himself be seized." However, a man is never released from the obligation to do his part in preparing for a break-through of the Divine. . . . Practice is nothing but work towards illuminating that power which separates man from life. It means the adventure of opening himself without fear, of hearing and heeding all the signs through which Being speaks to him.*
>
> **—Karlfried Graf Dürckheim**

The path of ecstasy is a path of transformation. That is, each of us needs to become capable of being God's lover. We need to become capable of deep appreciation of the world and fully receptive to the beauty and wonder that surround us. We need to learn how to fall in love with life and how to honor and celebrate the divine presence. We need to transform our resistance, resentment, and ambivalence to life, so that our response to God's proposal is not a tentative maybe but a wholehearted yes.

You would think that it would be easy to do the things that bring us ecstasy, but it isn't. In this society, we get rewarded for efficiency, productivity, and achievement, not for doing what makes us happy. If we don't go to work or pay our bills or clean the house, people will notice and there may be unpleasant repercussions. But who cares if we miss a yoga class we love or stop doing our morning meditation? If we don't take responsibility for our own happiness, for "following our bliss" (as the mythologist Joseph Campbell phrased it), nobody else will. Knowing what makes us happy isn't enough—we have to actually *do* it. We need to take that early-morning walk or that salsa dance class. In other words, we need discipline.

> *If ecstasy is the water of life, discipline is the bowl that allows you to raise that water to your thirsty lips.*

When you think of ecstasy, discipline is probably the last thing you think of. Doesn't ecstasy mean letting go, losing control? Isn't it just the opposite of discipline?

No. If ecstasy is the water of life, discipline is the bowl that allows you to raise that water to your thirsty lips. Many people know exactly what brings them joy, but they lack the discipline to follow through. Because they haven't crafted that bowl, they waste a great deal of precious time and energy.

If you listen to ecstatic music from any traditional culture, you'll hear some extraordinary drumming. As the singers cry out their longing, their praise, and their prayers, the drums express the underlying rhythms with impeccable precision. The drummer's discipline creates a foundation upon which the singers can soar and dip like swallows playing on the wind. In the same way, the disciplines we adopt should support rather than hamper our happiness and joy.

The word *discipline* comes from the Latin *discere*, which means to learn. So in the truest sense, discipline is neither a chore nor a form of punishment. It's the process by which you learn whatever it is you want to learn. If you want to become a great lover, for example, your discipline will encompass all the skills of good loving—the arts of romance, communication, seduction, and sex, for example.

Ecstasy is like a beautiful wild bird. You never know exactly when and where it's going to appear, but you do know that if you situate yourself in the right place and wait long enough, you stand a good chance of sighting your bird. Similarly, although we can't control ecstasy, we can make choices that put us in its path. Our disciplines should help us to do that. They should help us to cultivate an ongoing relationship with Spirit and they should prepare us to meet our divine lover.

So what might your disciplines be? When I asked my friends how they commune with Spirit, I heard an amazing range of responses. Here's a sample.

- Prayer
- Tai chi
- Yoga
- Tarot
- Journaling
- Rock climbing
- Spending time with animals
- Playing with children
- Hiking
- Reading spiritual literature
- Dancing
- Rituals
- Cooking
- Working with dreams
- Gardening
- Meditation
- Poetry
- Fencing
- Horseback riding
- Breathing
- Silence
- Flower arranging
- Pottery

The list could go on and on because our disciplines are as varied as we are. Many of my own disciplines are interwoven with my daily life. For example, I used to hate being interrupted by phone calls. So, to overcome my irritation, I started reminding myself, before I answered any call, that the caller is Spirit embodied.

When I remember that God or Goddess is approaching me in the form of this caller, I find it easy to greet everyone with love and respect.

Repressive Discipline

Many people discipline themselves and others in harsh, rigid ways. They might believe that this is for their own good, but in the absence of love, discipline never works. Discipline rooted in self-hatred is abusive and assaults the soul. "You're not good enough," it hisses.

Make sure that what you ask of yourself is a true expression of self-love. Loving discipline is like a violin string. If the string is too loose—that is, if you're too lax in your discipline—you can't make music. But if the string is strung too tightly, it's liable to snap. If we try to discipline ourselves without love, we get tense; sooner or later, the string snaps. We get to day four of a starvation diet, and then we break down and go on a binge. We exercise like maniacs for a couple of weeks, and then our resolution breaks down like an overheated engine in the desert. Some form of inner rebellion brings our elaborate self-improvement programs to a screeching halt.

People whose wills are extremely strong—anorexics often belong to this group—will stick to their chosen disciplines even though body and soul protest loudly. We sometimes admire and even envy highly disciplined people, but ego-imposed discipline generally does more harm than good and does not foster happiness. Ultimately, the soul's discontent will express itself, perhaps in the form of physical ailments or depression.

Unfortunately, religion has often misused discipline to repress and even torture the body. In India, I met a man who believed that the body was an obstacle to enlightenment, and who therefore held his

TRY THIS…

Sit down with pen and paper for about 10 minutes. Close your eyes and ask yourself the simple but all-important question, "What makes me happy?" Ask the question gently, as you would ask a friend you really loved. Ask with curiosity and a willingness to be surprised. Ask with an open mind. Write down whatever responses come.

Do this exercise repeatedly. You'll find that on different days, you get different answers—and that all the answers are valid.

right arm up in the air for countless years until it turned into a knobby, petrified flagpole, useless and immobile. "To reach God, one must transcend the body," he declared.

I bit my tongue and didn't tell him that I thought he'd been wasting his time, not to mention his poor body. His passionate but misguided quest reminded me of the folktale about a man who travels the Earth far and wide in search of a priceless jewel. Eventually, he learns that all the while, the object of his desire lay buried under his own hearth. This Indian ascetic never suspected that the body he so despised might harbor the priceless jewel of enlightenment.

In the West, such bizarre behavior is rare. But we, too, idealize self-control. Children who successfully control their impulses are admired and rewarded, whereas those who lose control often face humiliation, ridicule, and punishment. In school, children are taught to suppress their natural need to jump and run, climb and crawl, leap and skip, in order to sit quietly in neat rows like turnips planted in a dusty field. They learn to muffle their wails, shrieks, and squeals and to hide their true feelings. Ideally, school should help children to develop their strengths and skills. Yet all too often, it breaks the quirky, mercurial, wild colt spirit of a child with the bridle and saddle of repressive self-control.

The problem with repressive discipline is that it tends to backfire. People whose parents or teachers disciplined them in repressive ways may, in the end, have a hard time maintaining any kind of discipline. I once had a client, Tina, who lamented her inability even to take her heart medication every day. She swore that she really wanted to take her medication, but after just a few days, her firm resolution would get undermined by an inner rebel.

It turned out that the rebel was Tina's inner child, who had always experienced discipline as a form of punishment. She equated discipline with deprivation, withdrawal of love, and the violation of her essence. No wonder she balked. Tina's inner child had never had an opportunity to communicate her resentment. Instead, she expressed herself by vehemently rejecting anything that smacked even faintly of repressive discipline. The inner child needed to have Tina listen to her, validate her anger, and gradually win her trust by consistently loving and attending to her. Only then would Tina's inner child consider cooperating with any type of discipline.

The ecstatic's discipline is never anything but loving—in fact, love is the foremost discipline on this path. Whether we are Christians or Jews, Muslims or atheists, we cannot avoid the call to love. We should not act on any desire that offends the law of love—whether it is the desire to steal, to commit adultery, or to overindulge in alcohol—but instead, we should contain it with care and compassion. By acknowledging our more problematic desires as amalgams of positive life force and ignorance, we begin the work of purification that realigns our desires with the spirit of love.

Consider whether your disciplines are truly an expression of self-love. Do you actually feel loved when you perform them? Even such a minor discipline as brushing your teeth can be performed either mindlessly or as a conscious act of caring for yourself. Try it out. Next time you brush your teeth, wash your hair, or rub lotion on your body, allow yourself intentionally to receive your actions as a gift of love.

Boredom

Husbands and wives know that waking up and going to sleep with the same person day after day and night after night can be challenging. Relationships easily grow habitual and lose the exhilarating freshness of new love. The same is true in our relationship with Spirit. Without establishing certain routines, it is impossible to maintain the connection. Yet sometimes these habits trap us. We fall into set roles and create mental boxes that limit perception. Gradually, we lose the open-ended curiosity that lovers bring to their courtship.

Just like a human relationship, our relationship with Spirit, too, can become habitual and routine. Our challenge is to keep this love fresh and alive rather than allowing it to grow stale and predictable. Some people are proud of never having missed a day of meditation, but their practice resembles a safe, predictable conjugal visit instead of a tryst with an exciting lover. Making love is no fun if you do it the same way every time. Our spiritual lovemaking, too, should never become routine. It needs to stay vibrant and interesting.

Try to find the balance between discipline and creative freedom. Don't give up your discipline just because you're not in the mood now and then. On the other hand, if you continually find that you don't look forward to your spiritual practice, pay attention—you may need to change what you're doing. Remember that you're out to make love with Spirit. Let love inspire you, let pleasure bless you, and let your own creative genius show you the way.

The Adversary

Sometimes, you know that a certain discipline is rooted in love and would enhance your life, but some invisible force won't let you proceed. In this case, you may be dealing with what Christian theologians call the adversary. Jungian psychology views the adversary as an aspect of our shadow self—the dark side of the psyche. The adversary does not want us to be happy or to thrive. He or she does not want us to feel God's nearness or to experience ecstasy. Therefore, the adversary opposes the very disciplines that would make us feel happier and more fulfilled.

Sooner or later, every meditator encounters the adversary. You get up in the morning and think, "I really don't feel like meditating today." If this were a clear, conscious thought, you could question it, but more often than not, it's like a cloud that obscures your mind. By the time the cloud passes, you're sitting in your office, wondering what happened and why you failed to do something that you know makes your entire day go better.

"Get thee behind me, Satan," Jesus commanded when faced with the adversary. Jesus recognized Satan even when he appeared in the guise of a well-meaning friend. We, too, need to learn to recognize the adversary when he tries to undermine us (as he will, sooner or later), lest we act like gullible children and allow him to mislead us. Like the proverbial wolf in a sheep's pelt, he often claims to want only the best for us.

Why would Spirit install such a negative force within our psyche? I suspect that the adversary is to a spiritual seeker what weights are to an athlete. The adversary gives us something against which to test our strength, helping us to exercise our will and to build the muscles of our spiritual bodies.

When you notice the presence of the adversary, you might try acknowledging him or her respectfully, while firmly stating that you do not intend to listen to his or her advice or threats. Just as you feel ex-

TRY THIS . . .

What are your disciplines? List them all, large and small—brushing your teeth, taking vitamins, playing basketball, meditating, and so on. Consider the ratio of disciplines that support your physical well-being to those that support your mental and spiritual well-being. Do they seem balanced? Do you devote many hours a week to physical health but neglect your mental and spiritual development? Or are you a "heady" type who has no problem maintaining a daily meditation practice but balks at the idea of regular exercise? What would it take to balance out your disciplines, honoring the needs of body, mind, and spirit alike?

hilarated when you work out and realize that your body has gotten stronger, you'll feel extremely satisfied when you realize that you have the power to say no to this inner enemy. Moreover, you'll find that as you do so, the adversary's power will wane.

Choosing Happiness

We don't usually think of happiness as a choice, nor do we think of choosing happiness as a discipline. We assume that some people are just lucky and things go their way, or that they are born with a great capacity for happiness, just as others are born with blue eyes or curly hair.

But happiness is not just a gift that is dropped into our laps. It's more like a set of muscles. We're all equipped with them, but if we don't exercise them regularly, they'll never get strong. When we do exercise our happiness muscles—when we develop the habit of choosing happiness—they can transform our lives in amazing ways. When you choose happiness, you send the universe a signal: "I know that Spirit is here, and this knowledge gladdens my heart. I am open to even greater intimacy, greater pleasure. I am ready for ecstasy." Happiness prepares you to make love with life and it attracts Spirit to you.

In an article on love, the rabbi Harold Kushner wrote, "Some years ago I read a wonderful newspaper column. A woman sees two children in a playground get into a fight. One of them says, 'I hate you. I never want to play with you again.' For two or three minutes they play separately, and then they come back and start playing with each other again. The observer says to a woman sitting next to her, 'How do children do that? Be so angry one moment and together the next?' And the neighbor says, 'Oh, it's easy. They choose happiness over righteousness.'"[1]

If we want to have more happiness in our lives, we need to choose it. Sometimes, it descends unexpectedly, like a heavenly visitation. More often, however, happiness appears because we have invited it and have cultivated a habit of choosing it whenever possible.

Emotional Discipline

Choosing happiness is an aspect of what I call emotional discipline. Emotional discipline is based on the understanding that emotions don't just happen to us. We're not helpless in the face of our emotions; we have the power to work with them, amplifying those that support our happiness and minimizing those that don't.

Emotional discipline is different from repression. We don't deny what we're feeling. We do, however, take responsibility for our own part in generating emotions. For example, if we're grieving, we grieve fully for as long as we feel the need. Eventually, there comes a time when our grief no longer serves us. Initially, our grief was a healing force, but beyond a certain point, it becomes debilitating. If we have developed emotional discipline, we will watch out for thoughts that reproduce and perpetuate our pain. Instead of indulging in those thoughts, we will consciously discipline ourselves to focus on positive and healing images, thoughts, and words. We might, for example, chose a mantra, which could be a simple phrase such as "I rest in the arms of love," or even just the word *love*. Every time our minds return to thoughts that generate pain, we interrupt them gently by repeating our mantra.

Robbert's Story

I would like to share with you the story of a man who learned the practice of emotional discipline under extremely difficult and challenging circumstances. Although he had every reason to feel despair, he consciously and intentionally chose to feel happiness. We all know such people. They are ordinary heroes and heroines whose stories can inspire us to choose happiness for ourselves.

Robbert is a Dutch Jew who narrowly escaped the Nazi gas chambers by spending several years in hiding. After his initial flight from Amsterdam to a hiding place in the country, grief and depression descended on him like an avalanche, threatening to crush his will to live.

> I was 17 years old, and I had no idea whether any of my family members were alive. My hiding place was a small stable about 3 feet wide, and perhaps 8 feet long, and 6 feet high. If you think of a large coffin in which you can walk three steps and turn around and walk back, you get the picture. I had to suppress all my energy and keep it inside. There was a tiny window, about 10 inches

square, so I could tell when it was daytime, but there was not much light because the glass was painted blue. Dutch farmers believe that flies don't see blue light, so all the windows in farm stables are painted blue to keep out the flies.

A family lived in the house—a mother, a father, and four children—but for the first 8 months, the children had no idea of my existence. I was in a space nobody ever entered, and I had to be so quiet that the children never heard me. The woman of the house would tell the children that she was preparing food for the dog. She would put some food on a dog plate and leave it outside the door of my room, and I would open the door and bring it in. I didn't speak to anyone, I didn't hear anything, I had no contact with the world.

I spent nearly 2 years in that space. Later on, once I started working for the Resistance, I would come out at night every once in a while, but never during the day.

After I had been in this place for some time, I heard that all my friends had been executed and that my sister had been condemned to death. At that point, I fell into an immense depression. I was in terrible pain and could not stop crying. I am a very social person who has always loved being around people. I always felt that my purpose in life was to help people, to care for them. So I felt very lonely and very sorry for myself, here in this tiny room.

When there is no outside stimulation, you have no idea how to get out of such a state. How can I describe it? Imagine being trapped in an immense abyss perhaps a mile deep. You know there's daylight somewhere in the distance above, but you're in total darkness. You keep trying to claw your way up the sides, but there's nothing but sand to hold onto, and so the pit just keeps caving in on you. The harder you try, the more boulders from above crash down on your head, and you get more and more hopeless. That's how I felt.

I kept crying all the time. After a few days, I realized that I couldn't survive like this. I wouldn't make it through unless I managed to get out of this depression, but I had no idea how. Every time I tried I would feel more sorry for myself, more lonely, and in greater pain.

Gradually, I understood that I would never be able to help others unless I learned how to take care of myself first, and that I had to master my emotions. I had to prevent my sadness from overwhelming me because the moment that happened, I was lost. So first, I learned how to pinpoint the exact moment I started shifting into sadness. Immediately, I would tell myself, "No, that's not allowed, you cannot do that, you have to connect with your inner strength and think of positive things."

There came a moment when I realized that for a short time, perhaps 20 minutes, I hadn't felt the crushing depression. Maybe, I thought, I could handle the situation. Well, the moment I had that thought, I fell right back into my misery. So I discovered that I had to stay centered in myself without indulging in self-reflection, which would throw me back to square one, back into the darkness.

In this way, I gradually awakened to who I was and to the inner strength I possessed. I realized that by becoming centered in my inner power, I could enlarge myself and become bigger. Over and over, I had tried to climb out of that huge pit and had failed. But in the end, I grew larger than the whole abyss, like the genie in the bottle. I grew so large that the whole gigantic pit seemed tiny and insignificant, and the massive boulders looked like tiny pebbles.

This whole process took many weeks. During this time, I learned that as long as I stayed centered, I could cope with anything. I learned to control my fears and emotions, and I discovered that instead of just reacting to the situation, I could choose my emotional state. The moment I made that choice, I was free and able to be myself. In this way, I slowly became inwardly strong and stable.

Robbert credits this experience with giving him a foundation that has served him ever since. He knows, as few people do, that we are not merely victims of circumstances; we have the power to choose joy, to invoke it, and to cultivate it. "I can always become bigger than the situation," he says. "I have learned how to master myself, so my happiness doesn't depend on outer circumstances."

Expansion

Ecstasy appears naturally whenever the mind stretches and expands beyond its ordinary boundaries. Suddenly, you're aware of the sky in a new way. It's been there all along, but you hadn't noticed. You greet the moon and the stars as near and beloved friends. You feel both infinitely tiny and boundlessly vast; you feel as if you could hold the whole universe in the palm of your hand and lovingly kiss it. Your thoughts dissolve like clouds blown by the wind. "How can there be so much space within a head," you wonder, but then that thought, too, turns into a puffy white cloud and drifts away.

Sanskrit calls God *Brahman*, which means the everexpanding One. Although the ancient Hindus didn't have scientific evidence that the

TRY THIS ...

"Ask, and you shall receive" was one of Jesus' most radical statements. Most people don't believe him. But what if he spoke the truth? Ask for joy, and you shall receive it. Can it be that simple? Yes, it can.

Sit quietly for a half-hour, and with every breath think or say the word *joy*. As much as possible, keep returning to the thought of joy. Invite the angel of joy to enter you. Think about what joy feels like in your body, and what it feels like to be held in love. Let the word itself wash through you—that strange, indefinable, mysterious word, *joy*.

Notice how you feel in the hours that follow. Chances are that you will feel more joyful. Once in a while, the practice flushes out some undigested negativity, so you may experience a brief flash flood of grief, anger, criticalness, or even hatred. In that case, witness the feelings from as neutral a vantage point as possible, without judging their arrival as a bad thing. Instead, welcome them, allow them to stay as long as they need to stay, and release them as soon as they are willing to depart. This negative response to the joy meditation is quite rare, however. More often, you'll notice, either immediately or in the next few hours, a warm, generous feeling in your belly, a gentle radiance around your heart, or simple happiness bubbling up through your body.

universe was expanding, they saw God's expansive nature with their inner eyes. The 12th-century Zen master Hongzhi described the ecstasy of the expansive mind. "When the stains from old habits are exhausted, the original light appears, blazing through your skull, not admitting any other matters. Vast and spacious, like sky and water merging during autumn, like snow and moon having the same color, this field is without boundary, beyond direction, magnificently one entity without edge or seam."[2]

Mental expansion can happen spontaneously, but it can also be cultivated as a powerful ecstatic practice. Intentionally thinking expansive thoughts is an effective and time-honored way of preparing your mind for ecstasy. When you see yourself as a tiny speck of life on a tiny planet floating among billions of stars and galaxies, you may not get quite so upset when the cat vomits on the living room carpet or your sister-in-law is rude to you. It doesn't change what happened, but it does change your perspective.

Ecstatics love to explore the outer edges of things, such as the boundaries of the universe, billions of light years away, where science is forced to acknowledge its own limitations and pay homage to the awe-inspiring mystery that surrounds our planet. Just as the infinitely expansive cosmos offers fertile ground for ecstatic contemplation, so does the infinitely small world of quarks and subatomic particles that appear and disappear in response to unseen commands—a world in which specks of matter appear to know what is happening to other specks far away. Consider, too, the edges of time. If you sit quietly contemplating what preceded the beginning of time, you will feel the seeds of ecstasy germinating in your heart and mind.

There are many ways to expand. Look up at the sky more often. Go to a mountaintop or to any point that affords a long, expansive view. Watch the flight of birds. Contemplate your body's multi-billion-year history. Go out on a clear night and watch the stars. Listen to music that vibrates with infinity. Sit in a cathedral. Watch movies about faraway places. Meditate. Pray. Contemplate God as the ultimate frontier of all expansion. Ask yourself, "Who was I before I was born? What will happen to me after I die?" The importance of these questions lies not in the answers we give, but in the fact that they invite us to move beyond the limits of our lives and understanding.

Spend a few minutes thinking about the times you have experienced a sense of great spaciousness and expansion. What were you doing at the time? What led up to those moments? Would you like to have more of them? If so, what would it take? A walk in the woods? A day on the beach? A few hours of meditation?

Why not give it to yourself? Being productive, busy, and responsible all the time does not nurture the soul. Remember the question "How well have I loved?" Loving well begins with loving *yourself* well, and to love yourself well, you must now and then set your spirit free to soar in open space.

The Practice of Dying

Whereas ecstasy makes us wide and spacious, fear is a boa constrictor that insinuates itself into our musculature and then tightens its coils, contracting the fibers of the soft tissue into rigid bands. Because our greatest fear is the fear of death, death is a reality we must face squarely if we are to lead an ecstatic life. All the great ecstatics faced the fear of death and went beyond it. When the Indian mystic Tukaram attained enlightenment, he sang, "I saw my own death with my own eyes. What a celebration that was!"

"Life," the Zen master Suzuki Roshi once said with a gleeful grin, "means boarding a ship that's about to sail out to sea and sink." Suzuki's words may seem morbid, but he was only pointing out the obvious: The outcome of life—even the best life—is always death. To make love with life, we have to come to grips with the reality of death. When death becomes our friend, we have nothing more to fear—we have conquered the greatest fear of all. Isn't it ironic that preparing to die can heighten our enjoyment of life? Yet it does. Acceptance of death allows us to become fully present in life.

In *The Tibetan Book of Living and Dying*, the Tibetan Buddhist teacher Sogyal Rinpoche writes, "There would be no chance at all of getting to know death if it happened only once. But fortunately, life is nothing but a continuing dance of birth and death, a dance of change."[3] Dying is not just something we do at the end of our lives. Every day, we have countless opportunities to practice the art of dying. Someone yells at us unexpectedly—we tense, we feel resentful. Then we take a deep breath, relax, and let go of our tension and resentment. We might not think of this as the practice of dying, but any practice of letting go is practice in the art of dying.

The art of dying is one of the foremost ecstatic disciplines. This makes sense when you consider what death means: loss of control, surrender, letting go. The art of dying is the art of relaxing, which is the gateway to ecstasy. To die is to be released from a tightly confined form into a far more expansive, and therefore ecstatic, way of being.

How does one practice this art? The most important practice is meditation, which is the practice of presence. We can only be fully present insofar as we can let go of our past, moment by moment, let go of our future, let go of each breath, let go of all the thoughts that help us to weave a sense of identity. Therefore, meditation also teaches us how to die.

The second way we learn the art of dying is by intentionally remaining conscious of our own impending death. This is not the depressing practice you might expect it to be; on the contrary, it sets us free to live our lives to the fullest. Those who work with the dying know that dying people often radiate joy.

The Buddhist teacher Pema Chödrön tells the story of a woman who had been miserable all her life, but finally, at the very end of her journey, discovered her capacity to choose joy—proving that it's never too late to live an ecstatic life.

> As she grew older, she got more irritable and difficult. Then she got cancer and for some reason—after an initial period of resistance and anger—instead of getting more gloomy, she began to cheer up. The more she fell

TRY THIS...

Find some quiet, private time. Sit comfortably, with paper and pen handy. Close your eyes. Take a few minutes to settle down and quiet yourself by breathing deeply.

Imagine that you have been called to the deathbed of a very old person. As you approach, you realize that this person is you—a very old, very wise, very peaceful version of yourself. You are visiting yourself on your own deathbed.

Your older self is happy to see you and lovingly holds your hand. For a few minutes, you simply sit together in silence, breathing together and acknowledging the sacred passage that lies ahead. You notice that your older self is looking at you with great compassion. You wonder what your older self sees. What does your life look like from the perspective of one who has lived fully and is about to leave this world? At some point, the old one nods. This is a signal— it's time to gently open your eyes and pick up your pen.

Close your eyes again. Listen. Your older self wants to share with you the wisdom of one who is about to leave. Let the old one tell you about living wisely, living well, living joyfully.

Write down what you imagine your older self saying. Don't edit, don't question. Just write it all down. Whether it is just a word or many pages, accept it gratefully, without changing anything.

Nobody knows you as intimately as this person does. Your older self knows your hopes and fears, your struggles and your victories. Listen to this voice of compassionate wisdom. It can show you how to live fully, so that when your time comes to die, you will die peacefully, without regrets.

apart, the happier she got. She kept saying she was glad that she had this time to enjoy her life, which she had not enjoyed up to the moment that she got sick. Finally, the day before she died, she went into a coma. Everybody in her family, who were coming to feel more and more fond of her after all those years of finding her to be a pain in the neck, gathered around her bed crying and looking gloomy, just as she used to look. Just before she died, she opened her eyes to see them all standing there, and she said, "Gosh, you all look so unhappy. Is something wrong?" She died laughing.[4]

Although it may seem strange that an unhappy person would become happy just before her death, this is actually rather common. Much of our unhappiness grows out of our failure to relax into the present moment. When death is imminent, we finally let go of our fears about the future and our worries about pleasing other people. Instead, we give ourselves permission to simply be. And there, in that moment of pure presence, we find ecstasy waiting for us.

Author and teacher Stephen Levine was so struck by this phenomenon that he decided to experiment with living one year as if it were his last. In the book that chronicles his experiment, *A Year to Live*, he writes, "I wondered what this new aliveness was that we see so often in those with only a few months to live. What boundaries have been lifted so noticeably that previous hindrances to joy and mercy toward self and others melt into an increasingly expanding awareness and appreciation of the present?"[5]

The opportunity to spend time with dying people is a great gift. Being with dying people teaches us that death is not an enemy, but rather an opportunity to expand into the luminous immensity that is our true nature. James, a man in his early sixties, recalled moving into ecstasy as his wife, Kristin, lay dying of cancer.

I hesitate to talk about it because I loved her so much. How could I have been happy just as I was losing her? But I was. I don't know how to say this. The grief was ripping me to shreds, and at the same time, the joy was indescribable, beyond words. It was as if a part of me could see where she was headed and could feel this immense light that was pulling her in. I was so crushed by grief that I was wide open. I had no power or will to resist. And there it was, this incredible light. The memory of that joy sustained me in the dark times that followed, and I will never forget it.

Such stories are common. It seems that sometimes we can follow a dying person a little way on the journey, and catch a glimpse of the infinite love and the boundless ecstasy that the soul experiences as it returns home to its source. When her mother lay dying, the best-selling author and teacher Joan Borysenko and her son Justin were sitting at the old lady's bedside.

At about three o'clock in the morning, as we sat there meditating, I suddenly had a vision. I felt luminous, light-filled, and I felt that I was giving birth to the entire world in the form of a baby. . . . The next thing I knew I had left the consciousness of the mother and I was only in the baby, I was the baby and I was moving through a dark tunnel. I was born out into this tremendous realm of light—there are no words for what this is like, to say that you come into the presence of love, that it comes both from within you and from beyond you barely begins to sum it up. . . .

Then, everything about my mother and me became clear: that she had birthed me into this world and that I had just birthed her back out of it, that we were part of a circle of death and birth that went on forever.

I came out of the vision and when I opened my eyes I saw the entire room was filled with light—there was no place where one thing started and another thing ended, it was all molecules of light dancing. I looked across at my child, at Justin, and Justin was weeping. His face was suffused with light and he looked up at me and he said, "Mom the room is filled with light. Can you see it?" I said, "Yes, I see the light." And he said, "It's Grandma. She's holding open the door of eternity for us so that we can have a glimpse. It's her last gift."[6]

CHAPTER SEVEN

The Practice of Presence

If you are living in the past, you are not present.
If you are living in the future, you are not present.
If you are not present, who is?
Without you there is no intimacy.

—Emmanuel

There is such immense beauty in the human spirit. So much kindness, so much compassion waiting to be expressed. But often, these inner riches aren't shared until there is a disaster—a flood, an illness, an earthquake—that gives people permission to reveal their generosity and heroism. Emergencies enliven us, not because we are morbid, but because any reminder of life's brevity and fragility shakes us up and awakens us. Suddenly, we remember that the time to express love, to forgive, to be generous, to go out of our way to help others is *now*. So we do, and in doing so, we find great joy and satisfaction. We start to feel better about ourselves the minute we begin to live in the present moment.

"You must be present to win," say the casino signs in Reno. This is true in life, too. From the vantage point of the linear mind, the present moment looks like a meaningless blip sandwiched between eternities of past and future. But when you are fully present in the

TRY THIS . . .

Sit down in a quiet place. Take a deep breath. And another. And another. For just a minute, interrupt your train of thought and pay attention to your heart—that hardworking, underappreciated center of feeling. When you inhale, feel that you are offering this breath as a token of love to your heart. When you exhale, relax. Inhale life into your heart. Exhale and be at peace.

You will notice that after you complete an exhalation and before you begin the next inhalation, there is a tiny pause. Your breath seems to come to a stop. In that moment, an opening appears—an opening into stillness. An opportunity to be at peace.

Each inhalation and exhalation is like a journey. You leave home—that still point between exhalation and inhalation—and travel to distant places that fill your heart with love, and then you return to rest in the quiet refuge that awaits you between one breath and the next.

here and now, you discover a vast, luminous, inexhaustible field of being that spreads out in all directions like the universe itself. Those moments when everything glows with significance, when layer upon layer of meaning arises from the azure depths of the psyche, are always moments of total presence.

We live in a magical universe. Summer turns to fall, the geese prepare to fly south, and the pear trees groan under their load of ripening fruit. Everything in nature radiates the light of ecstasy, emanates the fragrance of ecstasy, and sings the song of ecstasy. All that we need in order to receive this bounty is to be fully present.

To be present means to be aware of yourself, moment by moment—to know what you are doing and experiencing. Most of the time, we're not here. We're thinking, but we don't know that we're thinking. We're breathing, but we aren't aware of it. We're driving in our cars, but mentally we're a thousand miles away. Let's face it: We aren't around for big chunks of our lives.

In any given moment, you might feel bored, sad, frightened, or excited. You might simply be aware that you are sitting in your chair, breathing and thinking and hearing the noise of traffic. Whatever you feel in this moment might not look anything like ecstasy. Nonetheless, it is your truth, and the truth is always a passageway to ecstasy.

Often, we resist being fully present in the moment because we're afraid of what we might find there—doubts, discomfort, boredom, perhaps grief. It's true that the practice of presence makes us more fully aware of uncomfortable feelings. On the other hand, the simple act of being present with these feelings is what allows them to change. The obstacles to ecstasy are like ice sculptures that, slowly but surely, melt in the warmth of our attention. In the end, only pure, luminous presence remains.

Radha's Story

When I first went to India, I was prepared to witness poverty and misery, but I was quite unprepared for the vitality and joy I found. Everywhere I turned, I saw laughter, giggling children, and broad smiles. I thought about how many downcast, hopeless faces one sees in Western cities, and I wondered why these people seemed so vibrant and happy.

I soon made friends with a young woman named Radha. She lived in a ramshackle hut, part of a slum that turned into a mosquito-ridden slough during the rainy season. Radha did not know how to read or write, and what little money she made selling flowers on the street was immediately spent on food. Nonetheless, she was a proud, self-confident young woman who refused to see herself as a victim of circumstances. Her joyousness amazed me. How could someone be so happy under such dire circumstances?

Over the next few months, I came to understand several things about Radha. First, I saw that as a member of a large extended family, she would never know the loneliness that so often plagues the poor and outcast in our country. Hers was not an ideal family by any means—for example, her father was a raging alcoholic—but it was nonetheless close-knit and loving. Also, Radha was very religious, and she celebrated with her community the many festivals that punctuate the Hindu year. Together, they would sing, perform rituals, and share whatever meals they could afford.

Spirit is pure presence. The journey of spiritual awakening and the journey of awakening to the present moment are one.

In Radha's eyes, I was the one to be pitied, because I had no husband, no children, and no nearby family. As far as Radha was concerned, family and community were the foundations of happiness. If she ever visited the United States, I suspect that she would find her beliefs confirmed: Loneliness is, unquestionably, one of the major causes of unhappiness in this country.

I do not want to idealize Radha's life, which was harsh and always threatened by the host of demons that accompany poverty. Nonetheless, she was a great teacher for me. Instead of responding to her poverty with anger or bitterness, she lived completely in the present, without worrying about the future. Laughter is free, and Radha laughed often and easily. Something was always triggering her mirth, whether it was the sight of a neighbor mock-boxing with a goat, the memory of something her little brother had said, or the way I mispronounced Indian words. Radha had mastered the ecstatic's most essential skill, the art of enjoying each moment to the fullest. Powerless over her outer circumstances, she had empowered herself to be happy from within.

God's Presence

Ultimately, Spirit is nothing other than pure presence. Therefore, the journey of spiritual awakening and the journey of awakening to the present moment are one and the same. The more you become present, the more you awaken to the presence of Spirit. Or, to put it another way, Spirit awakens to itself *through you*.

When the 19th-century mystic Ramakrishna was quite young, he served as a priest in a temple dedicated to the Divine Mother. Soon, he began to feel her presence everywhere, in all things. The temple managers, who prided themselves that all the rituals were performed impeccably in their temple, were horrified to discover Ramakrishna feeding the sacred food offerings to a stray cat, rather than to the Goddess. In response to their complaints, Ramakrishna explained, "The Divine Mother revealed to me . . . that it was She who had become everything. She showed me that everything was full of consciousness. The image was Consciousness, the altar was Consciousness, the water-vessels were Consciousness, the door-sill was Consciousness, the marble floor was Consciousness—all was Consciousness. I found everything inside the room soaked, as it were, in Bliss—the Bliss of God. . . . That was why I fed a cat with the food that was to be offered to the Divine Mother. I clearly perceived that all this was the Divine Mother—even the cat."[1]

All the great spiritual traditions assure us that if we were to live in unbroken awareness of God's presence—not just mental awareness, but full bodily awareness—we would live in constant ecstasy. An anonymous seeker described a moment of ecstatic awakening to what he called the living presence: "There came upon me a sense of exultation, of immense joyousness accompanied or immediately followed by an intellectual illumination impossible to describe. . . . I saw that the universe is not composed of dead matter, but is, on the contrary, a living Presence . . . that the cosmic order is such that without any peradventure all things work together for the good of each and all; that the foundation principle of the world, of all the worlds, is what we call love."[2]

We all yearn to know the living presence of Spirit as vividly as this man did. The thought of God is useful in that it opens us to the reality behind the thought. But in the end, it's not enough. We need the *experience*. Deep down, we need to know that we are not alone, separate, or cut off. Belief is a start, but ultimately, our souls demand firsthand knowledge. We get that knowledge by diving deeper and deeper into the present moment.

A Healing Ritual

We often think of Spirit as something outside ourselves, something other than ourselves. Eventually, we discover that what we seek lies within. To become present means to awaken to the presence of your own divinity and the divinity of the world. This is something we need to understand by the intuitive light of the soul, not just by the rational light of the intellect.

One such moment of awakening occurred in one of my women's circles. It centered around Tasha, a woman whose childhood had been a nightmare of abuse. The abuse had caused part of her psyche to split off from her conscious self—something common in severely traumatized people. On this morning, Tasha's long-repressed terror had risen to the surface to be acknowledged and healed.

Where Western psychology speaks of dissociation, shamanic cultures speak of "soul loss" and consider it the shaman's job to retrieve the parts of the soul that have left the individual's body. You might say, therefore, that we were involved in a ritual of soul retrieval. As

Tasha's midwives into life, we needed to summon all our love, skill, and focus to convince her traumatized child-soul to return. For a long time, we held her, rocked her, and sang to her as she lay on a blanket. Ever so slowly, our message began to sink in: The past had truly passed, and the present promised safety, joy, and love.

Eventually, the fractured part of Tasha's soul returned to her body. Still, I sensed that something more needed to happen.

"What is it that you want?" I asked her. For a while, she said nothing. Then she whispered, "Honor me. Honor me." And then, with a fierce strength gathering in her voice, she said, "I *will* be honored!"

Tasha was beginning to trust us enough to ask for what she needed. She needed to be acknowledged and welcomed, not just as a human being, but as a *sacred* being. The Divine Mother in us had welcomed her back. Now, the Divine Mother in her was demanding acknowledgment.

Tasha's clarity showed me what to do. Gently, I escorted her to a chair. As the women's circle watched in silence, I placed a candle by her feet and a radiant golden sunflower in her hands. Then, I invited the women to honor her in any way they wished.

What followed was one of the most beautiful and tender rituals I have ever witnessed. One by one, the women stepped forward. The first lovingly drew a soft red shawl around Tasha's shoulders, then kissed her hands. Others kneeled down and prostrated themselves before her. Some touched her feet, as people in India touch the feet of holy men and women. As Tasha quietly received our adoration and homage, her round face began to shine like the full moon, radiating peace, compassion, and joy. The more we honored her, the more her presence was transformed, until we all felt ourselves blessed by the embodied Goddess herself.

To one who has never experienced the divine presence embodied in human form, this may sound like blasphemy, but nothing could be further from the truth. We all knew that the object of our adoration could have been any one of us, or any human being. Had there been at that moment even the slightest trace of ego in Tasha or in us, the ritual would indeed have been blasphemous. But together, we had entered an altered state in which we were able to honor the sacred presence within ourselves and each other. Waves of ecstasy rippled through us as we celebrated the arrival of the Divine Mother in our midst.

Rita's Story

All too often, institutional Christianity has portrayed God as distant and unavailable. Sadly, many people feel that their chances of meeting God are about as great as their chances of having a long chat with the pope.

In my counseling practice, I often witness the terrible suffering caused by our collective denial of God's intimate presence. When Rita first came to my office, she was a very sick woman, both physically and mentally. In her 60 years of life, she had known little pleasure, let alone ecstasy. She had ignored her soul's signals of distress until her body's illness forced her to take note. Now, Rita's joints ached with unbearable pain and she could barely drag herself out of bed. "Chronic fatigue," her doctors announced, slapping a diagnosis on her that explained nothing and left her more confused than ever. Other symptoms appeared, including crippling bowel pains, blurred vision, and headaches. Determining whether Rita's depression caused her illness or vice versa was like trying to answer the proverbial chicken-and-egg question.

I knew that I was sitting with a woman who wanted to die and whose body was straining toward the final exit. Rita would undoubtedly die soon unless something changed her mind. I needed to find out where the roots of her despair lay. Why had she given up on life? At what point had she buried her hunger for ecstasy and decided that life was not worth living?

As Rita told me about her childhood, answers to my questions began to surface. Her father had been violent and full of rage, and had terrorized the whole family, including her weak, alcoholic mother. Rita was sent to a convent school where she was taught that she was a sinner who did not deserve good things. Moreover, she was told that life is a vale of tears and she should not expect to find happiness in the world, but God would reward her good deeds when she died and went to heaven. In her innocence, Rita believed everything the nuns told her.

I often witness the terrible suffering caused by our collective denial of God's intimate presence.

When Rita was 15 years old, her mother died. To say that Rita was heartbroken would be an understatement. When her mother passed away, a piece of Rita died as well. Although her mother had often let her down, Rita had known no other source of love. To make matters worse, Rita believed that her mother had died willingly. "She didn't exactly commit suicide," Rita told me. "It was heart failure. But I was really close to her, and I knew she wanted to die. Her life was intolerable and she felt powerless to change it, so she opted out."

The misery of Rita's childhood, her belief that her mother had chosen to die, and the messages she received from the nuns came together in the credo that had informed her entire life up to this point. In her eyes, the world was a place where God was not available. Death was the only ticket out of this godforsaken world and into a better one.

If you tell a child who hungers for divine communion that God despises this world, and if you teach her to think of God as a distant,

absent father—the type who is too busy to spend time with his kids—
her will to live is bound to shrivel. Now, many years later, desperate
and hopeless, Rita was standing at the very point at which her
mother had arrived prior to her death.

"What do you think about when you think of dying?" I asked Rita.

Through her tears, she replied, "I think of going to a better place,
a place where I'll join my mom."

"Rita," I responded gently, "how can you be so sure that the other
world, the world of light and love you long for, is somewhere else?"

Rita looked confused, so I told her a story about the death of a famous Indian teacher. As he was lying on his deathbed, his disciples came
to say goodbye, all weeping bitterly. The enlightened one opened his
eyes one last time, looked at them, and said, "Why are you weeping?"

"Because you are leaving us," the students cried.

With a gentle smile, he replied, "Nonsense. Where could I possibly go?"

"Rita," I continued, "You think of the physical and the spiritual
as two separate worlds, because that's what they taught you in Sunday
school. But what if they taught you wrong? What if that other world
is right here? What if it's just another dimension of this world, like a
radio station that you haven't known how to tune into?"

Rita nodded, hesitantly. "I think I get what you mean," she said.

Aware that Rita's mind was in that moment opening to a whole
new way of seeing, I pressed on. "Rita, can you imagine what
heaven might feel like? Give it a try. Close your eyes and describe
whatever you see or hear, as if it were right here, right now."

Rita had spent much time imagining and anticipating the afterlife, so this was easy for her. "It's full of light," she said. "I feel totally
safe and totally loved."

"Feel it as deeply as you can," I urged her. "Breathe in the light.
Breathe in the love. Relax into the sense of safety."

For the next 15 minutes, Rita explored this place of love and light
while I gently coaxed her to enter more and more fully into the ex-

perience. When she finally opened her eyes again, her face looked radiant and serene.

Gleefully, I pointed out that this heavenly place that Rita had always associated with life after death was actually accessible to her right here, right now, in the midst of *this* life. As the 15th-century mystic Kabir said, there's no point in waiting to meet the Beloved in some other world.

> *Friend, hope for the Guest while you are alive.*
> *Jump into experience while you are alive!*
> ·
> *The idea that the soul will join with the ecstatic*
> *just because the body is rotten—*
> *that is all fantasy.*
> *What is found now is found then*
> *If you find nothing now,*
> *you will simply end up with an apartment in the City of*
> *Death.*
> *If you make love with the divine now, in the next life*
> *you will have the face of satisfied desire.*[3]

Because Rita had assumed that there was no way to make love with the Divine in this life, she had begun to feel her way toward death. "That's how your mother did it," I said, "because she didn't know any better. She didn't know how to live an ecstatic life. But is it possible that you can do what she was not able to do? And is it possible that in healing your own life, you might extend a kind of healing to her as well?"

I reminded her of Jesus' words, "The kingdom of heaven lies within you." I said, "If you take those words seriously, Rita, they can change your life. They are a promise. They tell you that you can find happiness in the here and now. They invite you to embrace ecstasy as your birthright."

For Rita to experience the resurrection she needed, she had to stop conceiving of Spirit as external, as "out there," and begin to relate to it as an immediate presence "in here," a presence with which she could be on intimate terms every moment of her life. Instead of believing that she had to go to a different place to find ecstasy, she had to realize that all she needed to do was to open her soul to the realm of light all around and within her.

Slowing Down

If you came to me and said, "I want to have more ecstasy in my life. Please give me just one discipline to work with," I would tell you that presence is the doorway to ecstasy, and that the most useful practice for becoming present is slowing down. You cannot be present unless you move at the pace nature intended. The spiritual teacher Emmanuel said:

> *You human beings tend to be hurried and pressured*
> *and thereby deny yourselves the exquisite pleasure*
> *of savoring your lives.*
> *In this way, a great amount of joy*
> *and sweetness goes unnoticed.*
> *If life is lived with care and attention*
> *it will give you the sustenance*
> *and richness you long for.*
> *Allow yourselves to renew your commitment*
> *to your lives and to yourselves*
> *many times a day.*[4]

Rushing is stressful, but it's also addictive. We can get addicted to speed in the same way that we can get addicted to video games. Time becomes our opponent and the goal becomes cramming the greatest possible number of activities into the shortest possible time. Our minds can become obsessed with this game of control. We may believe that we achieve a lot when we rush around, but much of what we accomplish would be better left undone.

The Greek language has two words for time. The first, *kairos*, means sacred time—time that flows in harmony with the rhythms of the soul. *Kairos* is the soil in which all ecstatic experience is rooted. We enter *kairos* during good lovemaking or when we get so wrapped up in a creative project that hours pass like a single moment. Children are at home in this magical realm—hours with a beloved playmate flash by. Many so-called primitive people, too, live entirely in *kairos*. They have very few words in their languages to refer to the past or the future. Certain tribes from the rain forest have words for yesterday and the day before yesterday, tomorrow and the day after tomorrow—and that's it. Their lives float on the crest of a tiny ripple of time that rises out of a vast pool and almost immediately vanishes.

The second Greek term, *kronos*, is the root of our English word *chronology*. Kronos was a violent, angry Titan who devoured his own children. We have given our lives over to Kronos, who devours us, while *kairos*, sacred time, increasingly eludes us. As we rush around, we skim the surface of life without diving deeply into the dimensions of heart and meaning where the soul finds its nourishment. The Benedictine monk and author David Steindl-Rast tells us that the Chinese word for "busy" consists of two characters—*heart* and *killing*.[5] Busyness destroys not only the soul's joy in life, but the body's health as well. Stress-related illnesses are the foremost killers in our society.

Every so often, I send out newsletters to my clients. In one of them, I wrote a few paragraphs about our relationship with time. I noted the devastating impact of stress on our lives and suggested that cultivating a healthier relationship with time might be a key element in healing ourselves on all levels.

The response to that newsletter was amazing. Calls and letters poured in for weeks. People said that time pressure is one of the greatest causes of suffering in their lives. Many wrote about their longing to live in a more leisurely, gracious way and their frustration with the whirlwind pace of contemporary life. Clearly, my letter had touched a collective wound.

Our struggle with time and speed is a relatively new phenomenon. The watch was not invented until the 16th century, heralding a new in-

Silence, inner and outer, provides fertile soil for ecstasy.

dustrial era dominated by machines and by the rigid clock-time that machinery imposed upon workers who, until then, had lived with a shifting, fluid sense of time. Wristwatches were not worn until the 20th century, and I cannot help feeling that when we wear them, we mark ourselves as slaves of Kronos. Certainly, we have become slaves of time when we wind our way through rush hour traffic, repeatedly glancing at our watches, our impatience rising as we calculate our chances of making it to our next scheduled appointments on time.

Our situation reminds me of a scene in a documentary film in which a mother warthog was trying to protect her hoglets from a pack of hungry hyenas. Warthogs are large, powerful animals, and an angry mother warthog can do a lot of damage to a hyena, so the hyenas were cautious. Through the African dusk they came crawling, bellies close to the ground, eyes bright, instincts sharpened by hunger.

The mother warthog braced herself for battle; meanwhile, her babies sought shelter under her wide belly. But the hyenas demonstrated a mastery of strategic teamwork that disarmed the warthog entirely. First, two hyenas attacked from the right, provoking the anxious mother to charge. Immediately, others rushed forward from the left. As fast as she could, the warthog wheeled around to face this second threat. In the meantime, the hoglets were scampering around uncovered, and before you knew it, a hyena had an unfortunate hoglet clamped in its jaws. The hyenas quickly confused and disoriented the mother warthog so thoroughly that by the time they vanished into the night, she was left with only a single, terrified baby, the sole survivor among her litter.

I often think of that warthog when life's onslaught leaves me confused, angry, overwhelmed, and crazed. I start yelling at my phone because it won't stop ringing. Then my car breaks down. Just as I think I have everything under control, a friend calls and tells me that she has to have surgery, and there we are, facing the next hyena attack. I hear the same story from my clients—the committees, the business meetings, the dentist appointments, the personal crises, the kids, and on top of it all, our crazy mother-in-law announces that she's coming for a nice long visit.

The most useful practice for becoming present is slowing down.

Perhaps we are trying to outrun ourselves. If you stop running, you'll have to face your confusion, fear, emptiness, and loneliness. To slow down is to settle in with what is, to stop fighting it, to stop treating your life as an eternally incomplete remodeling project. This takes faith and a willingness to let go of the illusion that we can control life, keep bad things at bay, and secure the good. What will happen if we let our tight, worried grip on life relax? If we let go of the world, will God be there to catch it?

The Bible says that on the seventh day of creation, God rested. During my childhood in Austria and Germany, Sunday was indeed a day of rest. Stores were closed and very few people worked. The Muslim calendar, too, is punctuated with holy days during which all commercial activity comes to a complete halt—not to mention the five daily periods of prayer. Similarly, Jews celebrate the Sabbath as a day of sacred rest. The author and teacher Joan Borysenko fondly remembers the Sabbath ritual at the Jewish camp where she spent her summers as a child.

Each week, a different group of girls would be responsible for the celebration, and everybody would take a part. One of the girls would be the Sabbath queen, dressed all in white, and the others would be her court. She was the Shekhinah, the feminine face of God. The idea is that you are enfolded in the wings of the Shekhinah for these 24 hours out of time. We would have a procession leading to a pine grove by a lake, and all the girls would sing.

> *Come, O Sabbath day and bring*
> *peace and healing on thy wing,*
> *and to every troubled breast*
> *speak at thy divine behest:*
> *"Thou shalt rest. Thou shalt rest."*

And then there was silence. That was my first experience of meditation—that silent resting in the arms of the Sabbath. And we really did rest. There was no work done, it was all celebration and study. It was so joyful and beautiful.[6]

When I suggest that my clients devote a regular period of their week to *kairos*, sacred time, they often protest that they can't. "I'm just too busy," they say. "I don't have time."

"You *do* have time," I object. "You have 24 hours a day, and they're all yours. Don't blame other people and circumstances for how you spend your time. This is the most important discipline of your life. If you really want to experience greater peace and happiness, you must create an opening through which they can enter."

And they do, despite their jobs and their family obligations. It takes creativity and determination, but it's possible. One client decided that her Sabbath would be on Wednesday. Every Wednesday, she turns off her telephone and refuses to get in the car. The whole day is dedicated to the care of her soul and to the ecstasy with which her soul rewards that care. She cooks and gardens, meditates and drinks tea. Everyone benefits—she, her family, and the planet.

Meditation

Meditation begins with the practice of presence. If you don't yet have a meditation practice, consider starting one. There is no better, simpler, or more powerful way of keeping your mind open and un-cluttered in an increasingly cluttered and complex world. Like a musty mountain cabin, the mind needs to be swept clean and its windows flung open to the fresh, crisp morning air.

There are many ways to meditate. At its simplest, however, meditation is the practice of listening. Anytime we really listen, whether to the full-throated song of a thrush, the words of a friend, or the voice of the soul, we come home to the present moment. Therefore, any moment of deep listening is a moment of meditation. The practice of meditation strengthens our powers of concentration, enabling us to sustain our listening for longer periods of time. It also teaches us to give the gift of deep listening to ourselves—something many people find infinitely harder than listening to someone else.

To really listen, you must rest in your center. The Latin translation of "coming to the center" is *meditare*, from which the word *meditation* derives. Thus, our hunger for ecstasy leads us to the discipline of meditation, which is the art and practice of centering. When we rest in our center, the mind naturally falls silent, like a fox going to sleep in its den. Most religions recommend some form of meditation, but meditation does not require a religious context. We are all human beings who share a single source and a single center, no matter what we call it.

Meditation teaches us to take responsibility for our minds. We all know that we're responsible for what we do with our bodies. If we hurt someone or cause a car accident, we know that we'll be held responsible. The mind is a far more potent tool than the body, yet we don't usually hold ourselves responsible for what we do with it. "Well," you might think, "thoughts can do no harm." That's not true. Thoughts are immensely powerful. Every action,

good or bad, begins with a thought. Mother Teresa's life was based
on the thoughts she entertained, just as Hitler's was based on his
thoughts.

Like a perfectly centered pot spinning on the potter's wheel, a
well-centered mind remains calm and steady even as life whirls
around it. The larger the
vessel a potter wants to make,
the more precise the cen-
tering that is required. Beginning potters who have
not mastered the skill of cen-

> *To slow down is to settle in
> with what is, to stop fighting it.*

tering can't make very large pots. The same is true of the mind. Ecstasy is a state of great expansiveness. Everyone experiences moments
of spontaneous expansion, but we cannot maintain the state for long
unless we are firmly anchored in the center of our being.

If you ever have the opportunity to watch the whirling dervishes
perform their sacred dances, don't miss it. I can think of no more potent or magical image of perfect centeredness embodied. Like planets
spinning around the sun, like moths around the light, like a lover
around the beloved, the dervishes turn, uniting stillness and movement in perfect harmony.

Coleman Barks, a brilliant translator of Rumi's poetry, calls
this turning "molecular and galactic, and a spiritual remembering of
the presence at the center of the universe." He says that, according
to one story about the origins of the practice, Rumi "was walking
in the goldsmithing section of Konya when he heard a beautiful
music in their hammering. He began turning in harmony with it,
an ecstatic dance of surrender and yet with great centered discipline."[7]

Meditation is related to concentration, which literally means
"gathering into the center." What you gather into the center is the
fullness of your own presence. Any experience becomes clearer and
more intense when you are fully present with it. When you really

savor the taste of a raspberry, its flavor explodes in your mouth. When you really focus on a piece of beautiful music, it can bring tears to your eyes.

If we were madly, passionately in love with God, nobody would have to teach us how to meditate or concentrate—we would do it spontaneously. Love is like a magnet; whatever we love naturally draws our focus and holds it tight. When a man is in love with a woman, nobody has to tell him to concentrate on their lovemaking. When a child is playing a game she loves, she's perfectly present and focused. Whatever you love is so fascinating and so absorbing that it completely commands your attention—there's no question of getting distracted.

Like a perfectly centered pot on a potter's wheel, a well-centered mind remains calm and steady as life whirls.

The more we fall in love with Spirit, the easier meditation gets. Initially, however, our love for Spirit is usually lukewarm at best. We're interested, we're curious, we want to stay present—but our minds refuse to hold still. Some compare the mind to a butterfly flitting from blossom to blossom, others to a monkey leaping through the trees. I'm always reminded of a squirrel when I watch how my mind zigzags around in random patterns, nervously flicking its bushy tail, gnawing a nut here, burying another there, and promptly forgetting the spot.

Presumably, this habit of scattering our attention has deep instinctual roots encoded in our DNA. When you observe animals on the move, you see each species moving according to specific patterns and rhythms. The forward thrust of a grazing herd of antelope, the length of time a sparrow sits on a branch before hopping to the next, the complex choreography of bees—all these patterns are part of nature's plan to ensure the survival of the species. We, too, are animals, and both our minds and our bodies have deep instinctual urges to stay on the move.

Without sufficient discipline, the urge to run can overwhelm us at any time. My friend Martin told me about a time he entered a state of indescribable joy in meditation. "I never experienced such bliss before or since," he said. "But in the midst of this mind-blowing meditation, I suddenly remembered a phone call I was supposed to make. Before I could stop myself, there I was, walking to the phone. And that was the end of the ecstasy. I could still kick myself when I think about it. I've never been able to get back to the state I reached that day. And like an idiot, I cut it short." But Martin was no idiot; he simply succumbed to the mind's ingrained habit of staying on the move.

We speak of following a routine "religiously" because religion has often emphasized the values of discipline and regularity. Yet communion with Spirit should never feel like a chore. When you sit down to meditate, it should feel like the greatest luxury in the world. You are sitting down to bask in love. After all life's business, you are giving yourself the gift of total liberation: There is nothing you need to think about, worry about, or understand. Like a cat luxuriously draped before the fire, you are allowing yourself to rest in the healing light of love.

The Joy of Silence

When I sit in silence after a period of intense activity, I can sometimes feel my nerves humming like a beehive. As the silence envelops and permeates me, my nervous system calms down and becomes quiet. Muscles I didn't even realize were tense suddenly relax. My body heaves a deep sigh of relief. In this deep inner silence, I receive every experience deeply. Steindl-Rast writes of finding God within silence,

not only as perceived by the ears, but also a quietness inside, like the stillness of a windless midwinter day; brilliant with sunlight on virgin snow, the kind of day I
remember from my childhood in the Austrian Alps. Or
it's like the silence between a lightning flash and the
thunder crash that follows, the moment in which you
hold your breath. On an island in Maine I once found
tidal pools on the granite shore with water so still and
clear I could see the fine fibrils of sea anemones on the
bottom, waving like festive streamers. Still more limpid
is the inner space to which silence is the key. I don't always find that key, but when I do, I simply enter. Just to
be there is prayer.[8]

One of God's names is Silence—the great silence that contains all
sounds. Silence, inner and outer, provides fertile soil for the plant of
ecstasy. All sights, tastes, and smells seem clearer and more intense
when they arise out of silence, like the sharp cry of a goose piercing
the stillness of a winter morning. Therefore, the seekers of God have
always gravitated to places where outer silence supports the deepening
stillness within.

Silence lets the mind relax, expand, and become porous, allowing the light of truth to filter through its cavities and permeate
its shadowy depths. Only the silent, spacious mind, the mind that
has learned to stop talking and instead listen, hears the angels whis-
pering in the treetops. Only the silent mind hears the voice behind
the thunder and feels the caress within the wind. When we receive
an experience in inner silence, it becomes communion. We are in
touch with Spirit throughout the experience; we never disconnect.
Thus, silence naturally and spontaneously supports the blossoming
of ecstasy.

Inner silence, the sweetest fruit of spiritual discipline, equals the absence of ego, which cannot operate without the instrument of the thinking mind. In the absence of ego, we awaken to the divine presence. Spirit was showering us with love all along—yet in our distracted, unaware state, we did not notice. A haiku by the 13th-century Japanese Zen master Dogen evokes the ecstasy of Spirit's fullness flowing into the silent mind.

> *No wind, no waves.*
> *The empty boat*
> *is flooded with moonlight.*[9]

CHAPTER EIGHT

Beauty

If I had only two loaves of bread, I would barter one for hyacinths to nourish my soul.

—The Prophet Mohammed

If we are going to care for the soul, and if we know that the soul is nurtured by beauty, then we will have to understand beauty more deeply and give it a more prominent place in life.

—Thomas Moore

When you are fully present, everything you do is done with beauty. Your movements become fluid and graceful, and you relate to the world with skill, clarity, and care.

When you are present, you become more beautiful. You stay relaxed because you do not worry about the future or obsess about the past. Your face is open and your eyes shine.

When you are present, you drink in the beauty of the world around you. You appreciate details you would otherwise miss—the exquisite coloring of the sky, the quizzical expression on a child's face, the satisfying texture of the wooden table under your hands.

Our culture usually defines beauty in terms of individual taste. We forget that beauty is, above all, a spiritual quality. Beauty is ecstasy's twin: Beauty inspires ecstasy, and ecstasy opens our eyes to the beauty of the world. Indigenous cultures revere beauty and consider it a spiritual—rather than merely aesthetic—quality. Dhyani Ywahoo, a Cherokee teacher, says that in her culture, "the Beauty Path is one of right action, with consideration for future generations. . . . The person who has examined the nature of mind and relationships, who purifies the energy of anger, avarice, envy, and fear, and who dedicates actions for the benefit of all beings, such a person walks the Beauty Path."[1]

Mirror of the Soul

Beauty exists not merely to please the aesthetic sense, but also to lovingly remind the soul of its own light. If forgetfulness of our essence causes loss of Self and loss of joy, beauty is the medicine that heals our forgetfulness and restores our capacity for ecstatic experience. All beauty—whether the beauty of a person, an animal, a piece of music, or a landscape—acts as mirror to the soul.

Falling in love would not be the powerful experience it is were it not for the fact that the eye of love mirrors back to the beloved his or her innermost beauty. The first time Kabuo makes love with his wife in David Guterson's best-selling novel *Snow Falling on Cedars*, he says, "Tadaima aware ga wakatta. . . . I understand just now the deepest beauty."[2] Through his eyes, his beloved sees herself mirrored in a way that transforms her self-image.

Perhaps he is deluded, as lovers often are. Perhaps he is projecting a goodness onto her that she does not in fact possess. But more often than not, lovers perceive what others are too jaded to see. Their eyes penetrate to the soul, to the divine being hidden within the human. They mirror the best in each other, and in doing so, they call it forth.

In my book *Goddess: A Celebration in Art and Literature*, I tell the myth of the Japanese sun goddess Amaterasu. The story begins when

Amaterasu's brother insults her. Deeply depressed, the sun goddess withdraws into a cave, plunging the world into darkness and humankind into despair. "We'll surely die unless we find a way to brighten her mood," the people say.

Finally, they find a solution. When Amaterasu peeks out of her cave, they hold up a huge mirror to reflect her radiance back to her own eyes. Amaterasu is wonderstruck by the vision of her own light, and for the first time, she realizes her own magnificence. The more she looks, the more ecstatic she gets, until finally, she dances out of her cave and back to her heavenly home. Henceforth, the mirror becomes Amaterasu's sacred symbol.

Amaterasu symbolizes the soul, the inner sun that illuminates our lives. The message of her story is that the soul needs mirrors in which it can contemplate its own light. Without such mirrors, life's insults sadden and depress us. The light vanishes; everything turns cold and bleak. When that happens, we need to be reminded of how beautiful we really are. Ameratsu's ecstatic laughter is the laughter of the soul that sees its own luminous beauty reflected in the world around it.

Amaterasu is not the only goddess to whom mirrors are sacred. Mirrors are also sacred to Aphrodite, the Greek goddess of love and beauty, who is often shown gazing at her own reflection. Many of her sister goddesses, including the Yoruban goddess Oshun and the Hindu goddess Lakshmi, strike the same pose.

Commentators often dismiss this gesture of self-adoration as female vanity, but they miss the point. In Sanskrit, the poses and gestures of a deity are called *mudras*. *Mudras* are the ecstatic gestures of the cosmos, which contain hidden teachings and messages encrypted in the language of the body. A *mudra* should never be confused with a merely personal, ego-based gesture. Aphrodite is not Narcissus, the beautiful but vain boy who fell in love with his own reflection; she is the Goddess who creates the world and looks into the mirror of her creation with delight, proclaiming, "It is good."

What Aphrodite's pose tells us is that this whole universe is the goddess gazing at herself, Goddess beholding God, Spirit infinitely mirrored within Spirit. We too are the deity; through our eyes, Spirit looks, sees, and marvels. "Look at my world," the *mudra* says, "contemplate its magnificent beauty. Let yourself fall in love, knowing that what you see is the perfect reflection of what lies within you."

Our need for mirroring is inborn. Psychologists tell us that young children cannot thrive without positive mirroring—seeing themselves, through their parents' eyes, in a positive light. A child who is told that he is unlovable will believe what he hears, and his conviction will become a self-fulfilling prophecy. He may go through life feeling inferior and overly sensitive to other people's opinions of him, always hungry for the approval he never got as a child. But a child whose parents praise her and tell her that she is beautiful, smart, and lovable, will not only feel better about herself, she will actually *become* more beautiful, smart, and lovable.

As we mature, our need for mirroring doesn't cease, it just changes form. Assuming that we have developed a reasonably healthy, resilient ego, the mirroring we now require is of a spiritual nature. We need people who can see through the veils of our personalities to the clear light of our essential Selves, and who reflect that light back to us.

The Senses as Divine Messengers

When Jesus celebrated the Last Supper with his disciples, he told them that the bread they ate and the wine they drank were the body and blood of God. I don't think that he intended this ritual to be performed only during mass or communion. I believe that he was actually telling us that *anything* we eat or drink, touch or smell, is God's body. The road under our feet is God's body, the air we breathe is God's body, the food we eat is God's body, the body of our lover is the body of Christ, of the Buddha, of the Goddess.

When we consider communion in this light, we realize that Christ and Eros are not enemies but, on the contrary, beloved brothers. This was, in fact, what C. G. Jung suggested in a letter to Sigmund Freud, written in 1910, in which he called upon Christianity "ever so gently to transform Christ back into the soothsaying god of the vine, which he was, and in this way absorb those ecstatic instinctual forces of Christianity for the *one* purpose of making the cult and the sacred myth what they once were—a drunken feast of joy where man regained the ethos and holiness of an animal."[3]

> *Anything beautiful allows our senses to savor the sweet taste of the Divine.*

We receive more than just information through our senses. They pick up what in Sanskrit is known as *rasa*, which means juice, nectar, or flavor. *Rasa* is the flavor of God's presence. Anything beautiful—a piece of music, a painting, a beloved face—allows our senses to savor the sweet taste of the Divine. In an ancient scripture, the mystic rejoices as he drinks the wine of *rasa*. "Drunk am I by drinking the wine of Immortality which is your worship, perpetually flowing through the channels of the senses from the overflowing goblets of all existing things."[4]

On the path of ecstasy, we consciously enjoy the *rasa* of joy within all things. This spiritual juice is something we need as much—or more—than we need vitamins, minerals, proteins, and amino acids. Without it, our soul loses its will to live.

As a child, I used to sneak into Catholic churches and cathedrals. There, I would eagerly sniff the exotic perfume of frankincense and myrrh and watch the glint of candlelight on gold. Although I was not Catholic, I grew quite fond of the Catholic God. I figured that any god who was worshipped with music and incense, bells and flowers, sculpture and fine art, rich brocades and votive candles, and gold and jewels must surely be a connoisseur of all the finest pleasures life has to offer.

Catholicism is not unique in its sensuousness. All religious traditions celebrate the Divine with offerings of beauty. What could be more evocative than the stark elegance of a Shinto shrine or the exuberant beauty of a Tibetan temple? Step into the mysterious candlelit twilight of a Greek or Russian Orthodox chapel, where sheets of hammered gold cover the images of saints, leaving only small portholes for the hands and the serious, shadowy faces. The effect is strangely erotic, as when a beautiful woman covers her body, revealing only a flash of ankle. The saints' skin glows darkly in the candlelight and their eyes glint with fiery passion.

Throughout most of history, art was inseparable from religion. Art was understood as a sacred practice and a form of worship. An artist was someone who, having fallen in love with the world, felt called to create tangible mirrors in which people recognized the beauty of their world. What we call beauty is, in fact, our perception of God's presence. Beauty, in this sense, is inseparable from love, for the divine presence always inspires love, awe, and ecstasy. This is something the soul intuitively knows. Hungry for spiritual communion, it instinctively recognizes the sacred presence in the sweet face of a child, the music of Mozart, the grandeur of the ocean, or the loveliness of a woman's body, and knows itself nurtured and sustained by such visions of beauty.

Beauty is a lure that entices love. We know this intuitively, and so we try to make things beautiful for those we love. We buy fresh flowers or light candles. We bathe in fragrant oils and wear perfume, jewelry, and attractive clothing. To worship is to invite the greatest lover of all into our presence. It is only natural that we make ourselves and our environment beautiful to welcome the spiritual Beloved.

Zen Buddhism calls life the ultimate meal. If life is a meal, then the head cook is evidently hungry for beauty, for color, for spice and variety. Is it any wonder, in the face of this immense cosmic lust for sensual pleasure, that we too are born with the same need? Though our senses perceive only a tiny spectrum of reality—just the fraction needed to ensure survival—they convey valid information about

God's body, its textures and colors, smells and flavors. Despite their limitations, they are messengers that bring us tidings of the sacred presence and deserve our utmost respect and honor.

That the Spirit that created this world delights in all kinds of sensual beauty is obvious. Let us therefore embrace our own sensuality as an essential part of our spiritual nature. Worship should be a celebration—a feast of delight for both the soul and the senses. In worship, we awaken to the fact that we are the instruments through which Spirit enjoys the sensual pleasures of life. So why not come to your meditation cushion, your prayer mat, your temple or church or mosque prepared to meet your Divine Lover? Come as a lover comes to meet the beloved, full of joyful anticipation, with a trusting body, an open heart, and an eager, hungry spirit.

Adorning the Body

The priest and theologian Matthew Fox tells a revealing story about a Native American sun dance ceremony that he witnessed. In preparation for the dance, the young men were carefully tying orange skirts around their waists. One of them turned to the visiting priest and said, "I must look as beautiful as possible because I am preparing to meet the source of all beauty."

Matthew Fox was stunned. In all his years of preparing for mass and donning the ornate robes of a priest, no one had ever acknowledged that the reason priests decorate themselves in a ritual fashion is so that their own beauty will mirror and evoke the Divine.

I learned a similar lesson one night when I gave a lecture on classical Indian temple dance. This lecture was scheduled to include a 10-minute demonstration. Because the elaborate dance costume takes about 90 minutes to put on and equally long to take off, I reasoned that I would save myself that trouble and simply wear a colorful wide skirt.

TRY THIS...

Tomorrow morning, as you get dressed, try doing so with the thought that you are adorning and celebrating your inner Self. There is a world of difference between ego-based vanity and true care for the Self. As you put on your clothing (and makeup or jewelry, if you wear them), tell yourself that you are not disguising yourself, but rather revealing your inner beauty. Though you might perform the very same sequence of motions that you performed yesterday, the ritual will feel different.

After the event, an elderly Indian couple told me how much they had enjoyed the evening. "But you should have worn the costume," said the husband reproachfully. "When you dance, you become the Goddess. Putting on the costume is an essential way of inviting and honoring her. Even if you only dance for 5 minutes, you should always put on the costume."

All too often, when we attend to our appearance, we focus on covering up our blemishes. We feel that we are in need of improvement and that we need to disguise our flaws. How different we would feel if, instead, we focused on welcoming the God or Goddess within!

Our Failure to Honor Beauty

One of the tragedies of our times is our failure to honor beauty as a necessity. Although we enjoy it, we often consider it nonessential. In his book *Care of the Soul*, the Jungian psychologist Thomas Moore writes about this fundamental misperception.

In a world where soul is neglected, beauty is placed last on its list of priorities. In the intellect-oriented curricula of our schools, for instance, science and math are considered important studies because they allow further advances in technology. If there is a slash in funding, the arts are the first to go, even before athletics. The clear implication is that the arts are dispensable: We can't live without technology, but we can live without beauty.

This assumption that beauty is an accessory, and dispensable, shows that we don't understand the importance of giving the soul what it needs. The soul is nurtured by beauty. What food is to the body, arresting, complex, and pleasing images are to the soul.[5]

The Judeo-Christian God is masculine, and therefore Judeo-Christian culture holds all traditionally masculine attributes, such as power, control, and brilliance, in high esteem and considers them to be great spiritual virtues. In contrast, feminine attributes such as charm, grace, and sensuality supposedly have no spiritual merit. Though modern industrial society is nonreligious, it has absorbed Judeo-Christian values into its very foundation. It doesn't worship the biblical God, but it *does* worship his attributes, including power, control, and intelligence. Beauty, on the other hand, is considered a dispensable luxury. While industrial society acknowledges nature's charms, "she" is supposedly destined to be controlled, exploited, and dominated by mankind. The industrial world does not hesitate to destroy sites of great natural beauty, and since it doesn't perceive beauty as sacred, it is unaware of committing any sacrilege in doing so.

Treat the Earth like a whore, and she'll reflect our own inner ugliness. Treat her like a goddess, and her beauty will shine forth. In many places, our lack of reverence has created urban environments so unappealing and so offensive to the soul that people instinctively want to escape them. The more degraded the environment, the more we want to hurry through it. If people felt nurtured by their morning commutes, they would not be so upset about delays and traffic jams. By moving fast, they hope to avoid noticing both the disharmony that surrounds them and the inner discomfort it evokes.

I do not believe that the human race can survive unless we recognize the spiritual significance of beauty and make it a priority in our

The human race cannot survive unless we recognize the spiritual significance of beauty.

lives. Human beings need ecstasy, and ecstasy thrives on beauty. Whether we acknowledge it or not, the hunger for beauty is a basic human trait. To ignore it is to undermine the foundations of a healthy society, because in the absence of beauty, people fall into despair, addiction, and crime. The psychologist Ginette Paris writes, "I have often had the impression, when visiting deteriorated human settings, that real cultural poverty is expressed by the total absence of Aphrodite. In such environments, one cannot find a single splendid object, and everything that is nice, gracious, or fragile is sooner or later broken, tarnished, or ridiculed. There is a certain threshold beyond which ugliness and desolation threaten psychic survival."[6]

I once attended a meeting in my community concerning the pros and cons of allowing a fast-food chain to open a new franchise in a neighborhood that had, so far, successfully avoided urban blight. People talked about traffic patterns, congestion, and garbage disposal. Nobody mentioned beauty. When I talked individually to neighbors who opposed the franchise, it became obvious that their real concern was the ugliness of this particular chain's architecture. Yet, nobody dared to talk about beauty publicly. There seemed to be an unspoken consensus that beauty didn't count and that you didn't have the right to ban a business on the basis of aesthetic considerations.

A life without beauty is not worth living. Let's acknowledge publicly that beauty needs to be a prime concern of our city planners, our educators, our social workers, and our politicians. We need to stop treating beauty as the special domain of artists, and we need to stop dismissing art as merely ornamental. If we want to live ecstatic lives, we must live lives rich in both inner and outer beauty.

The Power of Natural Beauty

In the woods or mountains, by the ocean, or in the company of animals, we find mirrors that reflect the authentic Self—a Self that is innocent, pleasure-loving, radiant, and breathtakingly beautiful. Even the most elegant manmade environment can never rival the splendor of nature.

Whenever possible, I offer my workshops in rural places blessed with great natural beauty. I find that when I do, my job becomes much easier, for nature is an extraordinary teacher and spiritual guide. Every tree, every dewdrop, every spider web calls us to pay attention and rewards us with visions of exquisite harmony. According to an old saying from India, "What you meditate on, that you become." If you meditate on nature, you will become more real, more alive, more open to ecstasy, more yourself.

When our appreciation of beauty deepens into worship, we move into ecstasy. Beauty and ecstasy are as closely connected as thunder and lightening. The author Irma Zaleski writes of how, as a young child, her grandmother taught her to revere nature as a mirror of the Divine and as a gateway to ecstasy.

> I must have been five or six at the time. One night, I was awakened by my grandmother leaning over my bed. There was a noise of a great storm outside. Grandmother picked me up and carried me out onto a big verandah which ran all along the front of the house. "Look!" she said, and turned my face toward the mountains, "Look, this is too beautiful to sleep through." I saw black sky,

torn apart every few seconds by lightning, mountains
emerging out of darkness, immense, powerful, and so
real. Thunder rolled among the peaks. I was not frightened—how could I be?—I was awed. I looked up at my
grandmother's face and, in a flash of light, I saw it
flooded with wonder and joy. I did not realize it then,
of course, but now I do, that what I saw was *ecstasy*. My
grandmother was the first to point out to me a door to
joy.[7]

Everyday Beauty

We don't all live in beautiful environments. There is one kind of
beauty, however, to which every human being has access. This is the
beauty of life well lived. No matter who we are or what the activities
in which we are engaged, we all have the opportunity to create beauty.

This truth was made very clear when I visited a large museum
with an extensive collection of Greek and Roman art. Architec-
turally, the museum was impressive, with spacious, high-ceilinged
hallways that led into enormous, light-filled display rooms. As I wan-
dered down the hallway, I noticed a worker painting the walls. He
was working all by himself, and something about his air of total concentration arrested me.

I sat down on a nearby bench to watch, and immediately realized
that the man had already attracted quite an audience. With smooth,
elegant, almost catlike movements, the painter dipped his roller into
the liquid, a soft fawn brown. One perfect strip at a time, the shiny
wet color poured itself down, eclipsing the old, dull beige. Though
the painter was wearing blue overalls, he might as well have worn a
tuxedo, so spotlessly clean was his clothing.

Silent and completely entranced, the children in the room
watched his every move. I was struck that the spectacle we were now
witnessing—a human being performing a simple activity with perfect

grace, poise, and dedication—was as beautiful and fascinating as the world-renowned art displayed in this museum.

Music

The beauty of the intimate love play between Spirit and soul can never be adequately expressed in words. Over and over, mystical poets such as Rumi try, and then fall back into silence.

> *This is how it always is*
> *when I finish a poem.*
> *A great silence overcomes me,*
> *and I wonder why I ever thought*
> *to use language.*[8]

Music, with its capacity to move the heart like water flowing through reeds, is far better suited than words to expressing the exquisite play of tenderness and yearning, delight and wonder, that unfolds between God and the soul. Music can take a group of strangers and weave them into a single body faster than any other power can. More skillfully than any drug, it can whisk us off to paradise.

Music has always fed my soul, and some of my favorite memories of making love with God are musical. I grew up in a highly musical but adamantly nonreligious household, where it was more acceptable to believe in Santa Claus or the Easter Bunny than in God.

Yet Spirit is a trickster. Officially banished from our house, it sneaked back unnoticed, riding the waves of sound that poured out of our record player, hiding in the concert halls we visited, and sometimes even in my father's viola or my own violin. Mozart's sweet harmonies assured me that I had entered a loving universe, and the regal grandeur of Bach's fugues spoke of a cosmic order that combined meticulous precision with boundless generosity, compassion, and humor.

It was Indian music, however, that first awakened me to the powerful impact of music on our physiology. "Music," writes the author

TRY THIS...

Every day for a week, choose one simple activity, such as washing the dishes, getting dressed, or running an errand, and commit yourself to performing that activity with the utmost attention and care.

You may not think of yourself as a dancer, yet you are—your whole life is your dance. What will it take to make your dance graceful and beautiful?

If dancing well means slowing down (and it usually does), slow down. For this brief period, put beauty before efficiency and love before productivity.

The difference between sacred and profane dance is that the profane dancer is concerned only with what he or she looks like to others, whereas the sacred dancer is more interested in the inner experience of the dance. This chosen activity is your sacred dance. Don't worry what you look like. Instead, try to foster an inner sense of beauty.

Breathe deeply. It is nearly impossible to feel beautiful if you aren't getting enough oxygen. If you stumble or feel awkward, don't start criticizing yourself. Remember that beauty begins with love, and that loving compassion for yourself, just the way you are, is one of the most beautiful gifts you can give yourself.

Whatever action you choose, offer it as a tribute to life or as a prayer. I promise you that Spirit will gratefully receive your offering and reward you with an inner sense of satisfaction. When you give the world a gift of beauty, it rewards you with love.

Anne Lamott, "is about as physical as it gets: Your essential rhythm is your heartbeat; your essential sound, the breath. We're walking temples of noise, and when you add tender hearts to this mix, it somehow lets us meet in places we couldn't get to any other way."[9] Indian music, in particular, is designed to affect the listener in a visceral way. It reorganizes mind and body, transporting us little by little to the ecstatic realms where gods and goddesses walk among the stars.

Traditionally, an Indian music concert would start at dusk and continue until dawn. For both musicians and audience, it was a night of lovemaking. Today, even India has fallen under the dictatorship of time, and concerts there have grown shorter. Still, the music remains as sensuous as ever.

One memorable evening, I witnessed one of India's finest singers, Bhimsen Joshi, giving a 4-hour performance. As the rules of Indian music dictate, he began with a single drawn-out note, like a call to prayer. Again and again, his voice returned to that single note, sometimes tenderly encircling it, never straying far from it. For a long time, he continued in this way, using his voice to tune in to the spirit of the place and the moment.

Meanwhile, the crowd settled in like a flock of birds, ruffling their feathers, gradually quieting themselves, almost as if unaware of the powerful sound that was slowly penetrating their bodies, soothing their hearts, and calling to their souls.

This process of tuning in continued for a long, long time, binding us together in a web of magic. A Western audience might have grown impatient, but this audience intuitively understood the process and surrendered themselves completely to the voice of the great singer and the hypnotic trance he was casting. The world outside could have come to an end and we would not have noticed. Unhurriedly, calmly, a steady stream of healing sound kept pouring through us, Spirit calling to Spirit, soul to soul, until every last person in the audience was captured and entranced, all attention riveted upon his call.

Only when the singer felt satisfied that harmony prevailed on all levels, inner and outer, did he begin to play with the melody, slowly at first, teasingly, at times stroking and caressing with such excruciating sweetness that someone in the audience would moan. There could be no doubt that we were involved in a sacred erotic ritual, a ritual of ecstatic lovemaking. The singer was arousing and seducing us, although not in any explicitly sexual way; nonetheless, the air was thick with honey-colored light, the light of Eros, and heavy with the longing of so many souls, all turning toward their source like a field of sunflowers turning to face the sun.

CHAPTER NINE

Sexual Ecstasy

Love is often felt as sexuality.
Your body is an instrument of experience.
When you experience love,
you do so in your total physical being.
There is nothing within you, dear souls,
that is not designed to express love.
Sexuality is a wonderful door to openness.
It is the willingness to see and to be seen,
to share as completely as you are able
through each and every part of your dear self
so that you can be known and cherished.

—Emmanuel

$$L$$ ike wind and weather, sexuality is a force of nature. It is neither sinful nor immoral; it is amoral, just as the rain and the sun are amoral. The rain doesn't care whether it is ruining your picnic or saving your crop.

Nonetheless, even our crudest sexual desires are offshoots of the soul's need to know Spirit in the flesh. As the teacher Emmanuel says, "Sexuality is a biological doorway into truth."[1] Sexual love can transport us to the abode of the gods; when the body, heart, and soul move as one, we can fly across invisible thresholds into timeless dimensions.

Unfortunately, we often consider our sexual energy the least spiritual, least enlightened aspect of ourselves. When I say that sexual energy deserves our utmost respect and reverence, people are often surprised and even shocked. One day, as I was thinking about the sacredness of sex, I wrote the following story:

> Long ago, God told everything in creation what its purpose was to be. When the time came for sex to learn its purpose, God said, "You shall be a bridge builder. Between the world of Spirit and the world of matter, I have placed a wide chasm, deep and difficult to cross. Most human beings will cross that chasm only twice—at the moment of conception and then again at the moment of death.
>
> "I want you, dear angel, to build a bridge across the great abyss for each soul that is ready to be born. When I give you the signal, you are to escort the soul over that bridge and make sure it crosses safely from one world to the other."
>
> Sex bowed to God and said, "I am honored. But may I ask a favor?"
>
> "Ask!"
>
> "I ask not on my own behalf, but on behalf of your children the humans. To banish them entirely from your presence seems harsh."
>
> "Just for a brief while," interrupted God, "not forever."
>
> Undeterred, the angel of sex continued. "In your eyes, Mother Father God, a human lifetime is just the blink of an eye. But human perception is different. People are bound to forget where they came from, and they will feel lost and alone. Therefore, please give me the power to bring them back for a visit, now and then.

Let them have at least a glimpse of the paradise that is their true home."

God's heart melted in compassion. The Eternal One smiled and agreed. "So be it." Ever since, sex has built two different kinds of bridges. One helps baby souls cross over into our world. The other grants adults a brief sojourn in paradise. One gives us life, the other gives us ecstasy. Generous, compassionate, and mysterious, sex dances between the worlds, often scorned by humankind yet blessed by the Maker.

Sexual Communication

Traditionally, many marriages survived quite well without sexual communication. Men often took their sexual needs elsewhere, to a mistress or a prostitute. Women were expected to sacrifice their sexuality to their roles as wives and mothers. They succeeded so thoroughly that well into the 20th century, most men (and many women) considered women incapable of orgasm. In 1857, a well-known doctor by the name of William Acton declared with stunning confidence, "I would say that the majority of women (happily for society) are not much troubled with sexual feeling of any kind."

Fortunately, times have changed. Men and women enter into relationships with high expectations. They want pleasure, happiness, intimacy, and—yes—ecstasy. Most are willing to work hard to learn the skills of good loving, both sexually and emotionally. Among those skills, communication is the most important. If we want good sexual relationships, we need to learn to talk about our sexuality honestly. When you name your feelings, you bring them out into the open.

These days, we can at least seek out books for information, whereas most of our parents and grandparents had nowhere to turn.

Genevieve, a spry 70-year-old woman whose husband died 10 years ago said:

> It saddens me that I never had good sex with my hus-
> band, even though we loved each other so much. Maybe
> it was good for him, but I never had orgasms. At
> the time, I believed that was just something I had to
> accept, something I assumed every married woman had
> to accept. We never talked about it—it never even oc-
> curred to me to try. What would I have said? I was com-
> pletely uneducated about my own sexuality. Even if I'd
> known what I wanted, I would have been way too em-
> barrassed to say anything. Women didn't talk about sex,
> period.

Talk is healing. This is something I experience every day as a counselor and workshop leader. No matter how much you tell yourself that it doesn't matter whether you ever tell your sexual truth or not, it *does* matter.

Our stories contain medicine that becomes effective only when it is shared. In my book *Aphrodite's Daughters*, I asked women on the spiritual path to share their sexual stories. Hundreds of readers wrote to say that the stories they read there changed their lives and helped them to become whole. "I always suspected sex could be a kind of prayer," one reader wrote, "but I never talked about it—it just seemed too weird. Since reading your book, I've started talking to my husband. To my surprise, he's very open to experimenting. We're slowing down, breathing together, learning about the ways energy moves in our bodies. We're discovering a whole new world together."

Sobonfu Some, a teacher from the West African Dagara tribe, be-lieves that one of the reasons Western men and women have such struggles with their relationships is that they keep them too private.

"When everything is private and can't be talked about, it usually kills a relationship," she comments.[2] We need outside support, but we can't get it unless we talk honestly about what is going on.

By keeping silent about our sexual stories, we reinforce the belief that there is something shameful about our sexuality.

Children and teenagers in particular need to hear, not only about the physical aspects of sex, but also about the emotional and spiritual aspects. All too often, they believe that sex is dirty and sex talk even dirtier. Sexual words are handed around at school like contraband, smuggled furtively from one child to another. Few teenagers ever hear an adult talking about sex as something inherently beautiful and sacred. "You gotta be kidding," teenagers say when I tell them that in many cultures, sex was considered so sacred that certain religious ceremonies included lovemaking.

Deep down, most women and many men feel that they are "not good enough." Most of us live our sexual lives in airtight bubbles that insulate us from each other. We may have lots of friends, but we never discuss our sexual lives with them. Or perhaps we talk about sex, but only in a superficial, flippant way, always sidestepping our vulnerabilities and insecurities. By keeping silent about our sexual stories, we unwittingly reinforce the belief that there is something wrong or shameful about our sexuality.

Human beings need to talk. We have been talking for millions of years; it's one of the few things we do better than any other animal. For most people, verbal communication is an extremely important aspect of intimacy. How ironic, given our innate love of words, that so many of us never discuss our sexuality honestly or in depth.

Communication is the key to overcoming shame, which thrives

on isolation. Sexuality is an important and sacred part of our being, but we usually exclude it from religious gatherings. In my workshops, we very consciously and intentionally bring sex back into sacred space, from which it has been banned for so long. We talk honestly about our difficulties and challenges as well as our breakthroughs and victories. Piece by piece, we break down the barriers that fear has built. In doing so, we realize how many others share our supposedly personal problems.

Tantra

Tantra—also known as the art of sexual meditation—has become a popular practice in the West. Today, thousands of men and women use Tantric breathing exercises, rituals, and visualizations to channel their sexual energy. Tantra originated in India and was developed by both Hindu and Buddhist practitioners. It is one of the few surviving religious systems that use sexual energy to awaken the serpentine force or *kundalini*. Through a wide variety of practices that may, but need not, include sexual intercourse, *kundalini* is aroused, raised through the spinal column, and circulated through the entire body, giving rise to blissful states of ecstasy and expanded awareness.

In Tantric myth, God divides into god and goddess—Shiva and Shakti—who then create the world through their lovemaking. Shakti is the primordial Mother—in Latin, *mater* or matter. According to Tantra, matter is not really solid; it consists of pulsating energy that assumes an illusory appearance of solidity—a view strikingly similar to that of modern subatomic physics.

Our bodies, according to the Tantric view, are manifestations of Shakti. At certain points in the body, such as in the palms of one's hands or in the heart, the presence of the life force is easy to experience. The entire spinal column serves as a conductor for Shakti, who

TRY THIS . . .

Besides talking about sex, we also need to listen deeply to the inner voice of wisdom. Even if we have been told that sex is dirty or that our sexual bodies are ugly, there's a place inside where we know better—but we have to become very quiet to hear the voice that speaks from that place.

When you have a moment, invite Spirit to talk to you about sexuality. Sit down in a quiet place with pen and paper, and formulate a question you would like answered. Your question may be very general, such as "What is sexual energy?" Or it may be quite specific, such as, "What should I say to my 7-year-old daughter, who keeps asking me how babies are made?"

Spend a few minutes breathing deeply and simply inviting Spirit to be present in the room with you. When you feel ready, mentally ask for guidance and insight. Then, pick up the pen and allow Spirit to write a response to your question. Don't try to think your way to a response, just wait in an open, receptive way, allowing the words to flow through you and through your pen. Most people find that the voice of Spirit is far more easily accessible than they expected. If you get no response to your question, however, don't blame yourself or be discouraged. Simply try the exercise again some other time.

---

is called *kundalini* when she undulates through the seven main energy centers of the spine—the *chakras*, or vortexes of power—until she unites with her beloved Shiva in the crown *chakra*, the energy vortex located at the top of the head.

It's important to understand that traditional Hindu and Buddhist Tantra have little in common with what is currently known as Tantra in the West. Traditional Tantra is an austere, exacting spiritual path. Many Eastern practitioners of Tantra are celibate or work with explicitly sexual practices only at certain stages in their training. Although Western Tantra has drawn inspiration from its Eastern relative, the differences outweigh the similarities. The primary aim of Western Tantra is to heighten people's capacity for sexual pleasure by circulating sexual energy throughout the body, instead of merely discharging it genitally.

Astrid, a woman in her midforties, in describing her experience of Tantric meditation, conveys the ecstasy that this practice can inspire. "At one workshop I went to, we would sit together with various partners and meditate on the energy between us. With one man in particular, I found myself going into an incredible state of ecstasy. I don't think that I have ever experienced anything like that, even in orgasm. We weren't touching, we didn't even know each other's names, or care to—it wasn't a personal thing. It was orgasmic energy in the vastest sense. The ecstasy did not come from the personality level, but from the spiritual."

There can be no doubt that orgasm is an experience of ecstasy for the body. But the heart has its own ecstasy—its own form of orgasm, if you like—and so does the mind. It's a beautiful thing when the body's orgasm coincides with the orgasm of the heart and the mind. Western Tantra does us a great service simply by reminding us of this possibility.

Because I have studied certain Tantric practices and am interested in helping people access the sacred dimensions of their spirituality, I am often asked whether I teach Tantra. I don't. I do, however, teach people to approach sexuality as a meditative practice. In the following pages, I offer some pointers on the art of sexual meditation—or mystical sexuality, as I call it. These instructions represent no more than general guidelines. If you want to learn more about the subject, you may want to find a teacher with whom you can study.

Sacred Sex and Sacred Living

You cannot have mystical sex without acknowledging your partner's God-Self, and you cannot recognize the divine spark in another until you have discovered it within yourself. Therefore, the flower of sacred sexuality needs to be planted in the soil of a life dedicated to love in all its forms. Your sexuality does not exist in a vacuum, but grows out of your daily life. It will be sacred to the degree that your entire life is consecrated to love, compassion, integrity, and the process of awakening. Live a sensuous, pleasure-filled life, and chances are that you'll find sensuality and pleasure in bed, too. It's impossible to separate the practice of sacred sexuality from the practice of living in a sacred way.

Holiness is related to wholeness. When we are whole, we naturally intuit both the holiness of sex and the erotic nature of life. Whether we are stroking a lover's hair, the velvet moss that grows beneath a tree, or the soft fur of a cat, our touch will convey love and gratitude.

Like beauty, sacredness rests in the eye of the beholder—an eye that gazes upon all things with kindness and respect. When we relate to all things with reverence, then our sexuality, too, will be infused with love. If we honor and invoke the spirit of beauty everywhere we go, we will quite naturally do the same in bed. We cannot expect to go home and make great love with our partners if we don't know how to make love with a lake, a forest, the sky, the clouds, and the wind.

Gardeners don't grow plants; nature does. In the same way, there are no magic formulas for achieving sexual ecstasy, only tools and techniques for working with the inner flows of sexual energy. Resourceful lovers will discover many of these techniques on their own, and may spontaneously experience the ecstatic states that Tantric practice cultivates. Just as every gardener develops an individual way of working with water and soil, sun and wind, each person will find a unique way to relate to sexuality.

The Mystery of Female Sexuality

The best reason to practice mystical sexuality is for the joy of it, but there are other benefits, too. One is that it helps us to understand the nature of female sexuality and how it differs from male sexuality, an area in which our society is shockingly ignorant. Tragically, millions of women in their forties, fifties, and beyond accept the myth that attributes their loss of sexual interest to the aging process. They feel that they have lost their sexual spark and have become unattractive, asexual beings. In fact, this is far from true. Usually, the real problem is that sex, as they know it, doesn't touch their souls or reach deep enough to ignite their passion. What our culture considers normal sex might satisfy a 20-year-old man, but it is entirely inappropriate for most 50-year-old women.

"I'm bored with sex," Rosa, a woman in her late forties, confessed. But as we talked, it became evident that the truth was not quite so simple. Rosa was bored with sex as she knew it with her husband. He was, she said, a skillful and considerate lover, but still. . . . Her voice trailed off. Like many women, she had a hard time articulating exactly what she wanted.

"Do you have any sense of a different kind of lovemaking?" I asked.

She hesitated. "I don't know. But there's a feeling I sometimes get when we take lots of time. Like being under water. Like floating."

I told Rosa that I knew just what she meant. The floating, underwater feelings she so longingly described are typical symptoms of the altered state that lovers experience only when feminine and masculine energies are brought into balance. Chinese philosophy speaks of these energies as *yin* and *yang*. *Yin* is introverted and receptive, *yang*

(continued on page 182)

TRY THIS...

To enter the realm of mystical sex, you need a minimum of 2 hours, preferably longer.

At its best, worship becomes a way of making love with God. Similarly, sex at its best is worship. Therefore, let yourself feel that you are about to practice a form of worship. Take time to make the transition from your daily business into sacred space by taking a shower and relaxing. Remember that a tense body is not a sexy body. A sexy body is open, soft, and relaxed, like a cat basking in the warmth of a fire.

Just as you might place a flower or candle on your altar, you may want to prepare your room with flowers and candles. You can practice alone or with a partner who shares your interest. If you plan to practice sacred sexuality with a partner, you must be willing to approach your partner as the embodiment of the Beloved. This means that you must clear the air between you of any resentment or distrust.

If you practice alone, try to shed the shame associated with masturbation that many of us inherited. Remember Woody Allen's liberating comment, "Masturbation is having sex with someone I love."

Better still, call it self-pleasuring, since the word *masturbation* means, literally, "polluting with one's hand." Sexuality is one of the most beautiful ways we have of communicating love, not just to others, but also to ourselves. Just as a world of difference separates lovemaking from fucking, so self-loving takes you to an entirely different place than masturbation does. Instead of using your body like a prostitute, you cherish it like a lover and friend.

There is only one rule in this game: *Breathe, relax, and stay present.* The minute you notice yourself tensing anywhere, especially in your abdomen or pelvic area, stop. Breathe. Let go. As the saying goes, it's simple—but not easy. Unfortunately, we're conditioned to get tense and push toward orgasm. By tensing our bodies, we try to speed up the process by concentrating our arousal in the genital area. Try letting go of the need to climax, let alone climax quickly. This may sound frustrating, but you'll soon discover that the payoff is great. Your whole body will get aroused and saturated with pleasure, and you may find yourself entering an orgasmic state that is both deeply fulfilling and long-lasting.

Your breath is the gateway to ecstasy. It's a river that carries the life force to every cell. If you stop breathing during sex, the arousal will stay confined in your genital area. If you breathe, it will flow throughout your body. If you want not just sex but sexual ecstasy, remember that conscious breathing is the key.

Sexual fantasies can be great fun, but they don't belong in this practice. Do whatever you enjoy doing with yourself and your partner. But the minute you find yourself fantasizing, *stop, breathe, and relax.* Then start again. As you would in sitting meditation, try to stay as present as possible.

We're so used to tensing when we get aroused that at first we may feel thoroughly disoriented. "You can't have sex without tension," a friend recently told me.

"Yes, you can," I replied. "We're just so used to tensing that we can't imagine sex without it." You may also be surprised when you notice all the places you automatically tense up during sex. You may find that you don't know how to have an orgasm without tensing. That's

(continued)

TRY THIS . . . (CONT.)

okay. Remember, this practice isn't about having orgasms; it's about letting yourself stew in the electric soup of sexual energy.

In fact, when you get close to orgasm, try backing off. Stop stimulating yourself and ask your partner to stop, as well. Try to stay close to that line without crossing over it.

Sexual manuals often contain little diagrams that chart the path of arousal as a line that rises diagonally toward the moment of orgasm and then descends back down in a triangular pattern. The most fertile ground for ecstasy is the period just before orgasm, when desire is at its peak and one can sense the nearness of fulfillment. We know satisfaction is at hand—but we have not yet released the full energy of our desire. We are not empty, but filled to the brim with the most delicious sweetness, as if all our desire had turned to honey.

In sacred sex, we play with this edge. We learn to approach the crest of the wave without falling into orgasm, thus prolonging the period of ecstasy. See whether you can sustain the tension between wanting and not having for a little longer than you usually do. What's it like not to rush to get rid of desire? Take time to feel and honor your sexual energy without rushing to discharge it. After some time, you may feel tingling all over your body. This is a sign that you are moving into the orgasmic state. Try to stay in this state for an hour.

Have you ever walked along the crest of a hill with wide vistas opening up on all sides? This practice of balancing arousal and relaxation is like that. On one side lies the valley of orgasm, on the other the valley of complete relaxation. Your intention is to stay right on the cusp, balancing the two. If you practice as a heterosexual couple, the man must have enough stimulation to maintain an erection. At the same time, he will hold the balancing intention of relaxing deeply into the present moment without striving for release.

Any part of your body can enjoy sexual energy. Energy will move where your mind directs it to go. Experiment. Try channeling your energy toward your heart, using focused intention. Try sending it through your eyes into your partner's eyes. At first, you may not feel any results, but if you continue to practice, you will find that directing energy is easy.

Many men in our culture do not realize that orgasm and ejaculation are not the same thing. Through the practice of sexual meditation men can learn to enjoy multiple orgasms without ejaculating. This also means that they can learn to maintain their erections for long periods.

Certain Tantric teachings claim that men (but not women) should *always* avoid ejaculation because it depletes them of vital energy. They describe a man's semen as if it were a limited pile of coins that must be made to last a lifetime. It's worth considering the fact that these teachings were formulated for kings who had hundreds of concubines to satisfy. Unless you, too, have hundreds of concubines, I see no purpose in avoiding ejaculation entirely.

At its best, lovemaking merges great discipline with total surrender. Like any other art, lovemaking requires skill, knowledge, and practice. Don't think that if you just do what comes naturally, you will be a good lover. You won't. Stay humble, keep learning, and have fun.

is outgoing and radiant. Both sexes have both types of energy, but *yin* usually predominates in women, *yang* in men.

Biologically, a woman can conceive without orgasm, whereas a man must have an orgasm to impregnate her. Therefore, sex in its most primitive forms is very *yang*; that is, masculine energy prevails.

Good lovemaking shifts the balance by ensuring that the woman enjoys equal pleasure. Masculine energy still tends to override feminine energy, however. *Yin* is fine-spun, delicate, expansive, and therefore easily overpowered by the denser and more forceful *yang* energy. The type of lovemaking that most Western men and women consider normal, and which we see portrayed in the media, is actually very unbalanced, with *yang* predominating over *yin*.

This does not necessarily mean that the man is in charge. I am not talking here about male dominance, but about the tendency of masculine energy, in both men and women, to overwhelm the feminine. Some women have more *yang* energy than their partners. Generally, however, the imbalance affects women more than men, leaving them feeling shortchanged and unsatisfied.

Compared to ordinary sex, mystical or meditative sex has a far greater *yin* component. Therefore, if you are interested in meditative sex, the partner whose energy is more *yang* (usually, but not always, the man) should follow the lead of the *yin* partner.

The Dance of Presence and Desire

Our bodies are like batteries capable of holding a powerful sexual charge. Once the charge reaches a certain level, however, we seek to discharge it through orgasm. Nature has conditioned us that way to encourage procreation. Biologically, the main purpose of sex is to ensure the future of the species. And because procreation depends primarily on male orgasm, male sexuality—more than female sexuality— is dominated by the drive toward orgasm.

Just as mystical sex balances feminine and masculine, or *yin* and *yang* energies, it also balances restfulness and movement, or the relaxed enjoyment of pleasure and the drive toward orgasm.

Sitting meditation is perhaps the purest way to cultivate *yin* energy. Because our culture is so overwhelmingly *yang*, it's an enormously helpful practice for many people. In sitting meditation, we acknowledge desire when it arises, but we don't allow it to move us or carry us away. Meditation teaches us to sit with tension and discomfort without rushing to "fix" things.

When we are whole, we intuit both the holiness of sex and the erotic nature of life.

When we apply our meditative skills to lovemaking, we allow ourselves to truly feel our desire. We let ourselves get turned on, and then we just simmer in the energy. We don't run away from it and we don't push for orgasm. In this way, we begin to balance the arousal and drive of biological sex with the letting go and surrendering of meditation. Mystical sex balances presence and desire.

To be present is to be anchored in truth. Desire informs us of our power to co-create the future. In the practice of mystical sex, we honor the movement of desire and, at the same time, we remain firmly planted in presence. We try to let the dance of desire unfold without interfering—neither holding back nor pressing forward.

Over millennia, people have discovered that when one maintains this state of balance for a long time, something remarkable happens. As the sexual charge builds, it affects consciousness. A joyous, healing current sweeps through the mind, clearing out the cobwebs of fear and worry. The heart opens and the spirit soars. At times it may feel as if the body has no boundaries, but has dissolved into light.

When you raise the energy level in your body, where does it go? One of the most profound insights of Tantra is that energy will move wherever your mind directs it to go. Energy follows the guidance of your focused intention. If you direct sexual energy from your genitals to your heart, it will go there. If you visualize it moving up and out the top of your head, it will respond.

In Tantric manuals, you'll find diagrams depicting the pathways of inner energy. These are not maps in the literal sense; they merely describe possible routes you might try—routes that others have taken and found conducive to ecstasy. In this exploration, there is no right or wrong way. It is best approached as divine play, with a light touch and a sense of humor.

CHAPTER TEN

The Sacred Marriage

Jean and I have been married for forty-six years, and we have a kind of back and forth of feelings and intelligences, so that we've experienced "the one that is two and the two that are one." We do not have to theorize about it, we know what the hell it means. It's what Goethe calls the "Golden Wedding," and it is beautiful when that feeling becomes a fact in your life. . . . It is nice to know enough about mythology to realize how beautiful such an experience can be.

—Joseph Campbell

In traditional Western society, marriage to God and marriage to a man or woman were considered two mutually exclusive paths. If you wanted to seek God, you had to give up sex. In part, this rule reflected the church's view of sex as a spiritual pitfall. But we must also bear in mind that before the advent of reliable birth control, marriage was synonymous with parenthood—and usually, parenthood didn't mean having just one or two children. When you hear that the 15th-century mystic Margery Kempe had 14 children and almost died during several births, you can understand why she wanted to become a nun and kept trying to convince her husband to renounce sex (which he never did).

Even in an age of washing machines, microwaves, computers, and other supposedly time-saving devices, integrating two types of committed relationships—commitment to Spirit and commitment to a partner—is not easy. In fact, I think many married couples who are attempting this integration fail to give themselves credit for the magnitude of what they are trying to do. Spirit is no easygoing companion. On the contrary, as a partner, Spirit demands as much—if not more—of our time, energy, and attention as any man or woman.

Nonetheless, there can be no doubt that over the last two generations, intimate relationships have undergone a radical transformation. More and more couples view personal and spiritual growth as a central purpose of their relationships. They value their relationships not just as safe havens in a treacherous world, but as the best school in the art of intimate love.

"Relationships," writes Marianne Williamson, "are the Holy Spirit's laboratories in which He brings together people who have the maximal opportunity for mutual growth."[1] This is certainly not the attitude with which previous generations entered into marriage. Until quite recently, the purpose of marriage was to provide a stable and secure environment for family life. Mutual growth might or might not occur, but it was certainly not high on most newlyweds' lists of priorities.

Now, it is. More and more people are looking to love not only for security, but also for ecstasy. And because ecstasy is never found where Spirit is absent, this means that more and more people are approaching their marriages as spiritual practice. Without role models to show them the way, they are reinventing marriage from the inside out.

The Sanctity of Marriage

People who feel that marriage should be a lifelong, indestructible bond often complain that marriage is no longer sacred. But not all marriages *should* last forever. (I use the term *marriage* to refer to any kind of committed sexual relationship.) The sooner we discard the oppressive assumption that an ended marriage is a failed marriage, the better. If we approach relationships as opportunities for growth, it would serve us better to view the end of a marriage not as a failure, but as a milestone signaling that two people have reached the limits of their ability to serve as teachers for each other. It is time for them to bless the path they have traveled together and enter the paths they will henceforth travel separately.

If we judged marriages by their quality rather than their longevity, we might find that today, more marriages than ever before deserve to be called sacred. More men treat their wives as equals rather than as subordinates or servants. More couples are committed to the art of honest, respectful communication. Partners are less likely to put up with verbal or physical abuse and more likely to seek help when they encounter difficulties.

Choosing Wholeness over Security

Once you have experienced the joy of a loving, stable, committed relationship with Spirit, you never again enter into an intimate relationship because of need. Instead, you join with a partner to share the overflowing fullness of your being. Because you already feel loved in the deepest possible way, you need not use a human lover to fill an inner void. You know that ecstasy is not something another person can give you, but rather an inner fire that can, at times, be shared.

Knowing yourself married to God gives you a certain inner freedom. In your human relationships, you don't fall into the trap of making your self-esteem and your sense of your own value dependent on another's love and approval. You certainly are not likely to marry anyone just because you happen to be infatuated with that person, because the sex is good, or because that person offers you financial security. You consult your soul when making any major decisions, and you won't commit to a relationship unless you feel that Spirit supports it.

Over the years, I have had the privilege of meeting a number of couples who have been married many years and whose relationships continue to grow and deepen. All these couples have one thing in common. Although both partners treasure the marriage and have made great sacrifices for it, they put personal and spiritual wholeness first.

Making peace with our aloneness helps us build healthy, intimate, and enduring relationships.

Some partners have told me that at certain points during their marriages, they arrived at difficult crossroads. Conflicts arose—their partners wanted to do one thing, their own souls demanded something else. They knew that if they stayed true to themselves, their partners might leave. Surprisingly, they all took the risk of losing the marriage. Even more surprisingly, every one of them believes that doing so actually benefited the marriage.

"It's a strange paradox," Tony mused. In his fifties, Tony decided to quit his job and start his own business, a decision his wife did not support. This put an enormous strain on their marriage.

> I can't exactly explain it, but I felt as if I would die if I didn't do this. I had a good job and many people would have given their right arms to be in my place, but I wasn't happy. I knew that I was asking a lot of my wife—I went from a six-figure salary to having no income whatsoever overnight. But I also believe that if I had backed down, our marriage would have lost its juice and started withering away. I'm not saying that it wasn't rough. But we have an incredible relationship today, and I think that my sticking to my guns was important. My

advice is that if you have a gut feeling, act on it, because even though acting on it might cost you your relationship, not acting on it could cost you your soul.

Before we can have successful relationships, we must come to terms with the solitary nature of our journeys. Making peace with our aloneness helps us build healthy, intimate, and enduring relationships. The author Sam Keen tells the story of how, when he was pining for an unattainable woman, his friend and mentor Howard Thurman gave him a piece of advice he would never forget. " 'Sam,' he said, 'there are two questions a man must ask himself: The first is 'Where am I going?' and the second is 'Who will go with me?' *If you ever get these questions in the wrong order you are in trouble.'* "[2] God help us if we confuse our priorities and insist on having one particular companion throughout the journey. Keep your eye on the goal and trust that God will send you the company you need.

The moment we start believing that we can't be happy without a certain partner, we become addicts, little different than those who believe that they can't be happy without alcohol or cocaine. We may confuse the feeling of need with love, but need undermines the foundations of relationship. We do, of course, need human companionship, but when we start believing that among the billions of human beings on this planet, only this one can satisfy our needs, we cannot be totally honest. Because we believe that we cannot afford to risk losing this one person, we start censoring ourselves. But once we understand that Spirit is our primary partner and will never abandon or betray us, we can approach the challenges of human love with a lighter, less fearful heart. Our romantic relationships will be far healthier when we stop burdening them with unrealistic expectations and begin to appreciate them for what they are—sometimes ecstatic, sometimes mundane, always in flux, changing day by day as we ourselves change.

Successful relationships are often built on a shared sense of the sacredness of marriage. Psychologists interviewed 100 married couples. First, the researchers asked them how happy they felt in their marriages. Then, they asked the degree to which they experienced marriage as sanctified ("holy, blessed, inspiring, everlasting") and the degree to which they viewed marriage as an expression of the Divine. The responses to these two sets of questions were then correlated. The results?

> Seeing the divine either expressed in one's marriage or manifested in one's spouse correlated both with greater marital happiness and with a greater expectation of loss at the prospect of separation. Sanctification, it seems, makes emotional bonds stronger.
>
> While sanctifying one's marriage did not seem to prevent marital arguments (for the wives it slightly increased the frequency and/or severity of arguments), partners who sanctified their marriage were more likely to work together to solve their arguments and were less likely to resort to stalemating strategies such as sulking, giving the silent treatment, or withdrawing affection.[3]

It seems that our human relationships thrive when we make personal and spiritual wholeness our first priority. According to the relationship teachers Stephen and Ondrea Levine, "If our partners are what we love most in the world, we and our partners are in big trouble. If our partners are the people we love most in the world, and if God or the truth—whatever we choose to call it—is what we love most, then the relationship with those people is our most profound desire."[4]

Hannah's Story

Hannah is a woman whose strong commitment to Spirit helped her to recommit to her marriage of 7 years. Her husband felt very close to his two daughters from a previous marriage, and Hannah felt jealous and left out by the threesome. Worse still, she began to suspect that she no longer loved her husband.

Things went from bad to worse. Finally, Hannah separated from her husband and moved into her own apartment. She was fully prepared to get a divorce—in fact, she was looking forward to reclaiming her freedom—when she decided to see what would happen if she changed her attitude.

> For some time I had longed to go to Findhorn, a spiritual community in Scotland. Finally, I got a chance to go for 2 weeks. When I got there, I wept and wept for joy, not out of sadness. I really wanted to stay there and leave my marriage behind.
>
> Before coming to Findhorn, I had learned to ask for and receive inner guidance. I could tell the difference between mere thoughts and real guidance, which came as a kind of knowing that I had learned to trust. I tested it from time to time, and because I found it reliable, I decided to obey it implicitly. Every day at Findhorn I would ask about my marriage, and every day I got the same response: "You're not ready to hear this yet."
>
> On the last day, I asked again. This time, I was told, strongly and clearly, "You are to give up your apartment and move back in with your husband and his children. You need to tell the children the truth about your feelings toward them. Every day before you go home from work you need to meditate and get really clear, and you need to respond with total love to everything that comes your way." Then my inner guide added, "Don't imagine that you are doing anybody a favor. This is to show you what's possible in your life. At the end of 1 year, no matter

what happens, you are free to move out and never go back again."

I think that following this guidance was the scariest thing I ever did in my life, but I did it. I went back and talked with my husband, and he wanted me back. As soon as I could, before I lost my nerve, I talked to the children, who were teenagers at the time. I said, "At times I feel jealous of you when Daddy pays attention to you and not to me. I feel that I don't know you, and I want my own relationship with you. I don't want him in the middle between us." They thought that was great. Within 3 days, our relationship had turned around. My relationship with those children has become one of the most wonderful and precious gifts in my life. They are in their thirties now, and I love them deeply.

It was much harder with my husband. But by the end of the year, I was really, really happy. The previous year I had felt somewhere between suicidal and homicidal. Now, I was amazed at my happiness. I kept looking around me and thinking, "Nothing has changed except my mind, yet everything has changed." So I didn't want to leave. It was a very powerful lesson.

The question Hannah grappled with is one that we all face every day. How do we respond to our discontent? Sometimes, leaving an unhappy marriage, a home we've outgrown, or a frustrating job is exactly what we need to do. At other times, the true obstacles to happiness lie within. How do we know whether to focus on inner transformation or on outer change?

Hannah's response was to turn to the voice of Spirit within. To her amazement, the message from Spirit radically contradicted the voice of her conscious mind. A woman less spiritually committed might well have decided to ignore such challenging guidance.

Hannah, however, was truly married to Spirit and therefore trusted its guidance. Doing so not only saved her human marriage, but also strengthened her spiritual marriage immeasurably.

Three Ways of Integrating Marriage and Spirituality

Anyone can fall in love, but how many people are willing to take on the hard work required to stay in love? Men and women who have kept their love alive for decades know that staying in love requires nothing less than a total transformation of the ego. On a daily basis, they are challenged to disassemble their defenses, face unpleasant truths, and saturate the ego with kindness, humility, discipline, and patience. Having had a taste of paradise, they now have to practice the skills of building and maintaining love in the midst of daily life.

Good marriages aren't necessarily easy marriages. The fairy tales mislead us—very few people get married and live happily ever after. Most good marriages require a tremendous amount of work.

There are three basic, complementary ways in which partners can integrate commitment to Spirit with commitment to each other. Couples can use one, two, or—ideally—all three. I call them *the path of solitary practice, the path of partnership practice,* and *the path of the sacred couple.*

The Path of Solitary Practice

On the path of solitary practice, we have personal spiritual practices that do not involve our partners. We are cultivating two relationships side by side—one human, the other spiritual. We hope that the two relationships will complement and support each other, but they are nonetheless separate.

The advantage of this approach is that partners need not share the same spiritual beliefs or practices. One might be a Jew, the other a

Buddhist. One might not be interested in spirituality at all. I often hear people complaining that their partners aren't on the spiritual path. Yet as I see it, all human beings are on the spiritual path, whether they know it or not. Just because your beloved doesn't meditate or isn't interested in the same form of spiritual practice that you are, don't assume that he or she isn't spiritual. Some people find their spiritual connections in walking through the woods, some in work. Don't make assumptions about anyone else's spirituality, and don't fall into the trap of demanding that you and your partner share the same path.

Every human partnership is temporary. If a relationship doesn't end in separation, it will some day end with the death of one partner. Our relationship with Spirit, on the other hand, has no beginning and no end. Spirit will be your friend, companion, and lover no matter what happens. Therefore, it's important to cultivate your personal spirituality, independent of your partner. Doing so will help you feel a sense of autonomy within your marriage. And, as Hannah's story shows, the way of solitary practice can benefit a marriage in surprising ways.

The Path of Partnership Practice

In partnership practice, people sense that Spirit brought them together and that their love serves a spiritual purpose. Their relationship becomes a triangle, with Spirit serving as their mutual friend, guardian, and matchmaker. The author and teacher Sobonfu Some writes of the path of partnership practice, "There is a spiritual dimension to every relationship, no matter what its origins, whether it is acknowledged as spiritual or not. Two people come together because spirit wants them together. What is important now is to look at the relationship as spirit-driven, instead of driven by the individual."[5]

Besides sharing their spiritual practice, partners may also share some type of service-oriented work. For example, Sita and Bo Lozoff, who run the Prison Ashram Project, help inmates to use their time in prison for spiritual growth. Whether through active service or through shared spiritual practice, a couple involved in partnership practice experiences Spirit as a force that connects them, invigorates their marriage, and blesses their union.

Practicing as partners might simply mean speaking a blessing at mealtime, sharing the lighting of the Sabbath candles, or participating together in Sunday mass. One couple I know volunteers together in a soup kitchen once a month. Another performs a simple ritual every morning. Margaret touches Ben's feet, belly, heart, and head, and speaks whatever blessing comes into her mind, and then he does the same for her. The whole ritual takes no more than 3 minutes, yet Margaret and Ben say that those 3 minutes have become a treasured and important part of their marriage.

The Path of the Sacred Couple

The third way we can nurture the spiritual nature of a relationship is by honoring our partners as embodiments of the Divine. In the Hindu marriage ceremony, for example, husband and wife wash each other's feet as a gesture of reverence that acknowledges the divine presence in each other. This shared recognition of Spirit embodied in one's beloved is central to the type of practice I call the way of the sacred couple.

This third approach is foreign to many Westerners, especially to those who were taught that Jesus Christ was the only true son of God (something that Jesus himself never claimed), and that no one else should ever be honored as an embodiment of the Divine. Among the three ways of merging marriage and spirituality, the way of the sacred couple is the one with which we are least familiar. Because it can bring great ecstasy into a relationship, I would like to discuss it in somewhat greater detail.

Constellating the Sacred Couple

In the Brihadaranyaka Upanishad (an ancient Hindu scripture), a sage instructs his wife about the nature of the Self. The Self—as opposed to the personal self or ego—is the source of love. The small self divides; the great Self unites. The ego's job is to ensure our survival and well-being, which it does quite efficiently. It is, however, incapable of true love. The greater Self, on the other hand, the luminous, eternal ground of our being, *is* love. Just as the sun radiates light, the Self radiates love. Its love is neither sentimental nor fragile. Mood swings and physical ups and downs have no impact on it, nor does it fade with time. It is so real that it makes us gasp. It has the strength of a mountain and the gentleness of a feather.

The Self, the sage tells his wife, makes the marriage of two people sacred.

> *It is not for the sake of the husband, my beloved, that the*
> *husband is dear, but for the sake of the Self.*
> *It is not for the sake of the wife, my beloved, that the wife*
> *is dear, but for the sake of the Self.*[6]

What men and women look for in each other's eyes is nothing less than a revelation of the true Self, which, in Hindu terminology, is another word for God. This means that we look for glimpses of the Divine in our spouses. We love God through them, as they love God through us.

Viewing your spouse as divine may seem a tall order, especially once you are past the honeymoon phase and know each other inside out. You know his every foible and weakness. You have seen her at her worst and know how all-too-human she is. But if there's real love in your marriage, you have also caught glimpses of something extraordinary in each other—perhaps profound integrity, gentleness, strength, or a great capacity for forgiveness.

Whatever it is, don't lose sight of it. Treat it like a precious jewel and don't let it get buried under the everyday trash. That speck of beauty is the most real thing you'll ever see in your spouse, because it emanates from the soul. When we view our lovers as human embodiments of the Divine Beloved, there is no way we can be flippant or casual in our sexual involvements or justify dishonoring, abusing, or betraying those through whom the Beloved appears to us.

We all want and need to be treated not only with kindness, but also with reverence and even devotion. The divine presence within us wants to be seen and acknowledged. Therefore, if we want to offer our partners the kind of love they crave and deserve, we must discover the radiantly beautiful masculine and feminine within them. When a man has true love and reverence for the feminine Spirit, and a woman for the masculine Spirit, this goes far toward supporting their relationship's integrity.

When we fail to perceive the divinity within our partner, we get stuck in ego-based vision. Criticism, defensiveness, and power struggles take over. It is therefore very important that we consciously refocus our perception every day, so that we stay in touch with our soul and our lover's, and with the love that blossoms when two souls connect.

Whenever we approach our partner as the Beloved, we constellate the ancient archetype of the divine couple, God as a couple united in perfect love. World mythology abounds in such couples—Isis and Osiris, Inanna and Damuzi, Shakti and Shiva, to name just a few. We lost touch with this immensely joyous and healing archetype when we banished the Goddess and made God an asexual male. Is it any wonder that men and women in our culture have a hard time understanding one another? By reclaiming the image of the sacred couple and meditating on it, we pave the way for healthier and more harmonious relationships.

In every marriage, partners will get on each other's nerves and bicker and argue. The question is whether they can keep their love alive. The only way to do that is to keep looking through the ego to the soul. At the level of soul, we are all breathtakingly beautiful. If you know how to perceive the soul within yourself and others, you'll fall in love with your husband or wife again and again. The ecstasy we all seek in love, and so often lose over time, *can* be kept alive, but

(continued on page 200)

TRY THIS . . .

This is a practice for couples. Sit facing each other in a quiet place where you won't be interrupted. Make sure that you have at least 45 minutes. Mentally affirm that you intend to perceive and honor the Divine within your partner. Determine which one of you is going to be the timekeeper in this practice. The time-keeper needs a watch and some form of bell, which could simply be a glass and a fork.

Get comfortable. Close your eyes and breathe deeply. Feel yourself relaxing. Try not to drift off into thoughts of anything ex-traneous. Instead, try to be fully present.

After about 5 minutes, begin to think of your partner without opening your eyes. Entertain the idea that underneath your partner's changing personality, there is something constant, an essential quality of being that this person was born with and will die with. We can call it the soul.

How does one perceive another person's soul? To see the soul, one must look with the eyes of love. Set aside your critical, analytical mind and allow yourself to feel your love for this person. Breathe love through your body until you feel it viscer-ally, in your heart and belly. Feel how deeply you desire happi-ness and well-being for your partner.

Now, allow yourself to become receptive to any impressions of your partner's soul that may arise. People most commonly receive such impressions in three ways. First, ask yourself what essential qualities you associate with your partner. Examples of essential qualities are compassion, gentleness, playfulness, joy, radiance, power, grace, clarity, and generosity. Second, you may get impres-sions of certain colors and shapes that reflect this person's essential being. Finally, you may find symbols or images arising in your mind—an oak tree, a clear crystal, a gentle deer, a queen, a priest.

Whatever images, words, or impressions arise, just notice and receive them gratefully, without analyzing them. If no specific qualities, colors, or symbols emerge, that's fine, too. Simply focus on your love for this soul and send it your blessing.

After 10 minutes, the timekeeper should gently strike the bell, indicating that it's time to open your eyes.

Now, take turns sharing what you felt or saw.

Remember that essential qualities are always positive. If you saw fear or anger in your partner, this is not the time to discuss such perceptions. Your job is to look beneath the fear and anger to the soul and to honor its luminous beauty. Whatever you say to your partner should come from pure kindness and generosity.

Please listen to what your partner says to you without commenting, interpreting, or trying to initiate a discussion. Your job is simply to receive your partner's words in the spirit of love. When your partner has finished speaking, thank him or her.

When both of you have spoken, end the practice by bowing to each other or hugging.

When partners share this meditation together, it goes a long way toward strengthening their love. You can also do this practice on your own, however. I have witnessed amazing changes in relationships after one partner started meditating on and blessing the other's soul, even though the other was unaware of being blessed in this way. The soul seems to sense when it has been seen and honored, even when the conscious mind does not.

to do so, we must keep clearing our vision, so we can see our loved ones with sacred eyes.

Martha's Story

I worked with one couple whose marriage was wonderful in many ways. Nonetheless, the wife was contemplating divorce. Her husband, she said, was a good friend to her, but not a good lover. "I so long to be swept off my feet by a great passion," she told me. "I've never experienced that and, with my husband, I doubt I ever will."

My work with Tom focused on improving his skills as a lover. Meanwhile, I asked Martha to explore the source of ecstasy. Martha longed for ecstasy, yet she clearly viewed it as something a man had to give her—otherwise, she couldn't have it. When her husband failed to give her ecstasy, she felt enraged and let down. Although she saw that her anger damaged the relationship, she couldn't help herself.

Martha's crisis was less sexual or marital than spiritual. All her life, Martha had longed for communion with Spirit, and all her life, she had imagined that romantic love would satisfy her longing someday. Now in her late forties, she was getting desperate and was asking herself whether she should have an affair. But the real question was whether Martha could access her inner source of ecstasy. Her marriage to Tom (or anyone else) would not work until she cemented her marriage to Spirit.

We all want to be happy, but we aren't always sure where the source of happiness lies. Every spiritual tradition in the world tells us the same thing: The source of happiness lies within. *Ecstasy does not enter from the outside—it shines from the inside out.* No matter how often we hear this truth, we all forget it. We begin to believe that the source of happiness is money or success or being loved by other people.

For many months, Martha and I explored the terrain of her soul. Gradually, she began to contact the Divine Mother and then the inner

Lover. Typically, our spiritual evolution needs to follow this sequence—we need to experience parental love before we become ready
for sexual love. Adults who were not loved as children are challenged
not only emotionally, but also spiritually. They may feel alienated from
God, without knowing ex-
actly why. The archetypal
figure of the Mother is often
the key to the sense of intimacy that spiritual communion requires. Once they find
this key, whether through

*Every spiritual tradition tells us
the same thing: The source of
happiness lies within*

psychotherapy or through spiritual work, their intimacy with Spirit
grows rapidly.

Martha, whose mother had been emotionally and physically abusive, found that meditation on the Divine Mother helped her to grow
confident in her sense of being lovable, worthy, and desirable. On
this foundation, her love affair with Spirit could unfold.

Although Tom's skills as a lover have improved, he is still no
Romeo. Nonetheless, Martha is very glad that she did not leave him.
Much of what she hoped to receive from him she now receives in
her spiritual practice. Instead of demanding that Tom be her god, she
accepts him as the imperfect yet exquisite human being he is. Instead
of venting her frustration on him, she appreciates his loving devotion. To her surprise, his sexual skills improved greatly once she
stopped burdening him with expectations he could never fulfill. Tension, seriousness, and fear have given way to a delicious sense of light-
ness and laughter.

Why Nasruddin Never Married

No human relationship is perfect, and we kill our marriages when
we can't accept their imperfections and flaws. A Sufi story about the
beloved fool Nasruddin makes this point beautifully.

Once, Nasruddin's best friend asked him why he had never married. Nasruddin scratched his head and said, "Well, I wasn't going to settle for anything less than the ideal woman. First, I found one who was beautiful and wealthy, but stupid. The second one had a mind as sharp as a silver dagger, and all the wealth a man could desire, but she was not beautiful. And then. . . ."

"What then, Nasruddin?"

Nasruddin sighed deeply. "Well, finally I found the perfect woman. She was more beautiful than a summer garden, she had a heart of gold, a keen wit, and wealth to boot."

"So," asked the friend, "why didn't you marry her, if she was so perfect?"

Nasruddin shook his head sadly. "Woe is me, my friend. It seems that she was looking for a perfect man."

CHAPTER ELEVEN

The Power
of Community

> *Without a community you cannot be yourself. The community is where*
> *we draw the strength needed to effect changes inside of us.*
>
> **—Malidoma Some**

Buddhism talks about the "three refuges" that are available to every spiritual seeker. The first refuge is *sangha*, which means community in Sanskrit. When we speak of community, we usually mean a specific group of people whom we know and with whom we spend time. In a larger sense, though, all beings belong to our community—those we don't know, as well as those we do. We are like molecules of water in a great river, all interconnected, each flowing into the other. Community is not just something we experience when we come into physical contact with others. We are always in community, even when alone. We share community with all beings in the same way that we share the Earth.

Like most religions, Buddhism acknowledges that we are not intended to make the spiritual journey in isolation. No matter how much we love and enjoy solitude, there comes a time when we must reconnect with others. Alone, we can get only so far in our practice. Alone, we never become aware of our blind spots. Alone, we may get discouraged and lose faith. Alone, we may lack the inspiration that would keep spiritual practice fresh and vibrant. Most important, we have no opportunity to share our gifts when we are alone.

The best way to learn the art of ecstatic living is to join with others who are doing the same. My workshops have taught me the power of the domino effect. When you witness the stunning beauty of a person surrendering to Self, and when you bask in the glow of the joy that follows, you grow impatient with your own prison bars. "If she can break free, perhaps I can, too," you think. And with adequate support and encouragement, you can.

To create spiritual community, you don't need to be a "spiritual expert" who has all the answers. If you're clear in your intention and willing to experiment, Spirit will show you the way. A friend of mine realized that she longed to pray with others. But she didn't want to pray in a specifically Christian or Jewish or Hindu way. She simply wanted to open her heart in compassionate love in the presence of others who were doing the same. So she started a prayer group with four friends. The group has been going for more than 4 years and has grown as more people joined.

The Purpose of Spiritual Community

A spiritual community is a connecting link between humanity and Spirit. It's a giant ear that can hear the voice of Spirit better than one lone individual can. And it's a vessel capable of containing a far greater spiritual power than a single person can hold. When we invoke Spirit in community, we have access to an immense source of power.

We were all born with a longing to be witnessed and a deep pool of spirituality that demands expression. Spiritual expression can take many forms—song, praise, prayer, tears, even rage. We need connection with others who share our hunger for Spirit and who can assure us that we are not crazy for feeling as we do. We need to know that underneath their polite, controlled masks, others feel as passionately about life as we do.

Most places we go, we're seen as persons who perform a certain type of work, as mothers or fathers, or as people who are rich or poor, beautiful or ugly. When we come to our spiritual community, we need to be recognized as embodiments of Spirit. Like beauty, spiritual community should mirror the soul's ecstatic essence.

Every person has gifts that need to be given to the world. We each bear the responsibility to give of ourselves, but we also need community support. Our spiritual community must insist that we share our gifts and help us to do so. There is nothing more tragic than someone who never finds a way to share his or her riches—and we all have riches of one kind or another.

The most important purpose of any spiritual community is to initiate spiritual communion. If it does not do that—if it allows itself to get bogged down in politics, in social activities, or in organizational work—it has outlived its usefulness.

Going to Jerusalem

Atum O'Kane, a Sufi teacher, tells a story about ecstatic community that he heard from the story's protagonist, Shlomo Carlebach, a Jewish mystic known for his ecstatic singing.[1] It's a story about our hunger for ecstasy, our fear of it, and the power of community.

One day, Shlomo was flying to Jerusalem, where he had a community fairly close to the airport. As the plane approached Jerusalem, he felt more and more ecstatic. For Jews, Jerusalem is not just a physical place, but the center of the universe and the archetype of the holy city. To go to Jerusalem is to move into sacred time and space. So Shlomo was having a difficult time containing himself—which is what often happens to ecstatics.

As he looked around, he saw a young girl of 8 or 9 sitting nearby. He could see from the spark in her eye that she knew what it meant to go to Jerusalem—not just physically, but in the deeper sense.

He leaned over to her and asked, "Have you ever been to Jerusalem?"

*I*t's *been so long since we experienced the joy of spiritual community that we have almost forgotten what an oasis it is.*

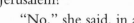

"No," she said, in a tone full of great wonder.

He said, "Oh. Let me tell you about Jerusalem." As they talked, they both became more and more ecstatic.

But suddenly, the girl's father leaned over and said sternly, "I don't think this is appropriate."

Shlomo looked at the mother and father, and the best way he knew how to describe them later was as Mr. and Mrs. Sour Cream. He could see that they knew nothing about the inner Jerusalem. He also had a feeling it had been a long, long time since there had been any real warmth between them. He didn't want the girl to feel caught between him and her parents, so he withdrew. But for the rest of the trip he kept thinking, "She really knows what Jerusalem means. What can I do to welcome her when she arrives?"

Just as they landed, Shlomo had an idea. Because he had an Israeli passport, he was able to clear customs much more quickly than Mr. and Mrs. Sour Cream and their daughter. Shlomo knew the chief of the Tel Aviv airport redcaps, the porters who carry people's luggage. Shlomo also knew that all the members of his own community would be coming to greet him with their musical instruments and drums. So Shlomo asked the head of the redcaps, "Can you do me a favor?" and whispered his plan in the man's ear. Immediately, the chief called a strike of all the redcaps in the airport.

The members of Shlomo's community were waiting to greet him, and as he cleared customs they started playing their instruments.

Shlomo started singing and all the redcaps started dancing. The red-caps weren't carrying any luggage, so activity in the whole airport came to a stop while all the travelers crowded around the singers and the dancers.

Soon, Mr. and Mrs. Sour Cream and their daughter came through customs. They had lots and lots of luggage. They looked at this spectacle and the husband got angry and yelled, "Only in Israel would this happen!" But while he was getting more and more furious, other people, including many of the passengers, were joining the singers and the dancers, and they, too, were moving into ecstasy.

Once things were going full tilt, Shlomo called over one of the children of his community and said to her, "See that girl? Go and dance with her." Soon, the daughter of Mr. and Mrs. Sour Cream was laughing and dancing just the way David danced before the ark.

At first, Mr. and Mrs. Sour Cream seemed frozen in horror as they watched their daughter dance. But then, something shifted. Mr. Sour Cream put his arm around Mrs. Sour Cream, and she put her arm around him. After the singing and the dancing had ended and Shlomo had offered a blessing, Mr. Sour Cream threw his arms around Shlomo and cried. He said, "It has been so long, so very long."

In this way, Shlomo welcomed the family to Jerusalem.

I love this story because it's true, and because it shows how Shlomo held a space for Mr. and Mrs. Sour Cream to overcome their fear, acknowledge their longing, and join the circle. I suspect that many of us could say, with Mr. Sour Cream, "It's been so very long."

Meetings in Sacred Space

Most people have no spiritual community at all, let alone one that values and supports ecstatic experience. Many of us live like camels crossing an endless desert. It's been so long since we experienced the joy of spiritual community that we have almost forgotten what it feels like to arrive at a welcoming oasis. I've met countless people who left their spiritual communities in exasperation. "We no longer were receiving the spiritual nourishment we needed," they tell me. But when I ask where they now go to worship, many shake their heads sadly and say, "Nowhere."

If ecstasy is indeed a spiritual experience that is triggered by communion with the Divine, one would expect our communities to provide ecstatic celebrations for young and old. Our churches, temples, and mosques would be centers of ecstatic dance, prayer, and worship. But most religious centers discourage ecstatic communion. Why are there so few positive examples of ecstatic community? Why do we so rarely gather to pray, worship, and celebrate in a spirit of ecstasy? I have no answers to these questions, but I believe that they need to be asked.

Traditionally, people have looked to religion to satisfy their need for spiritual ecstasy, but many religious organizations have become too rigid to serve the needs of the living soul. This situation presents us with an opportunity to explore fresh, supple forms of spiritual practice. Instead of starting with tradition, we could start with questions: What do we need? What would best serve our souls, our communities, and our planet?

The name of my workshops, "Meetings in Sacred Space," reflects my answer to that question. As you may recall, the word *ecstasy* literally means "to cause to stand outside." Because we step outside of our egos when we enter sacred space, creating sacred space is one of the great ecstatic practices. Though I am by nature a very private person who shies away from parties and large groups, I go to my circles as a Christian goes to church, a Jew to temple, or a Muslim to the mosque. I do so because I believe that, in our time, we all have an urgent need to create spiritual community. Together, we can access Spirit far more easily than we can individually. Without spiritual communion, we have no chance of transforming our world the way we must if we are to survive, let alone doing so in a spirit of grace and joy.

Moreover, without spiritual community, we tend to burden our romantic relationships with impossible expectations. We expect our partners to inspire and entertain us, to heal and nurture, to listen and understand—not just now and then, but whenever we need it. I've seen people become so wrapped up with their intimate partners that they stop nurturing their relationships with themselves and with their communities. Their list of priorities looks like this.

1. Feed the relationship.
2. Nurture myself.
3. Connect with my community.

If your list looks like this, too, I suggest that you turn things around. Your first priority should be nourishing yourself. Second, strengthen your sense of community. Third, nourish the relationship.

People are often surprised that I put community ahead of relationship and marriage. I do so, not because I think intimate relationships are unimportant, but because I believe that they can't thrive unless they are embedded in supportive community. I've seen too many potentially good marriages fall apart because each partner needed the other to be everything at once—best friend, lover, therapist, financial adviser, and general assistant. Having isolated themselves, the couple had no community to help them sort things out and to support them when the marriage started cracking under the strain.

The Jungian analyst Jean Bolen says that we are not human beings on a spiritual path, but rather, spiritual beings on a human path. In sacred space, that is how we look at each other—as spiritual beings on a human path. We might be confused, scared, or sad, but each one of us is also magical, mysterious, and miraculous.

When sacred space is established, we begin to speak in a more honest, authentic way. We express thoughts and feelings that we never even knew we had. We also begin to listen more deeply. Just as a bird-watcher in a tropical rain forest listens for the unique call of a certain bird, in sacred space we listen for the voice of the soul, which is a voice of authentic truth. When we hear it, we welcome and support it. When we don't hear it, we wait patiently. Given the opportunity and the right circumstances, even the wariest soul will eventually emerge. It might take a long time before a person feels safe enough to express authentic thoughts and feelings, but in sacred space, there is no sense of pressure. We lovingly accept people as they are, all the while holding an opening for their growth, always beckoning them toward that opening.

> *When we gather with a sincere intention to relate with love, reverence, and soulful listening, we enter into sacred space.*

The most important prerequisite for creating sacred space is clear intention. When we gather with a sincere intention to relate to ourselves and others with love, reverence, and soulful listening, we naturally enter into sacred space. Sacred space is not lofty or pompous. It doesn't require a temple or special clothing. In fact, it has nothing to do with outer space at all, but with inner space. If Shlomo Carlebach's community could create a sanctuary in the middle of the Tel Aviv airport, we can do it anywhere.

I have learned, over the years, that groups are as individual as people. Each group has its own personality, its own agenda, its own gifts, challenges, and tasks. My task, as the facilitator, is to help the group as a whole and each person in the group to arrive at a point where the mental chatter falls away, allowing the quiet voice of the soul to be heard. To bring the group to that point, I might use music and dance, ritual and storytelling, meditation and silence. Once the group is there, it's up to Spirit to reveal itself, and up to each participant to open both heart and mind to receive what Spirit offers.

Group Mind

If you spend enough time in sacred space, you can't avoid noticing that our minds are connected and can work as one. Group mind is a common, ordinary phenomenon. To see it in action, you need only observe a flock of birds flying in formation or a line of ants harvesting food. Watch how they move in perfect coordination, each individual sure of his place and purpose in the whole. Group mind is part of our evolutionary legacy as human beings. Eons before we discovered the gift of speech, we used empathy, intuition, and psychic insight to stay connected.

Many people find the phenomenon of group mind scary. We have been taught to perceive ourselves as separate individuals and to dismiss psychic phenomena, telepathy, and other symptoms of mental communication as hocus-pocus. On the one hand, we discredit the possibility of group mind. On the other, we're afraid that it could sweep us away and drown out our individuality.

Group energy is indeed powerful. Therefore, whenever we open into a larger field of energy, we need to ask ourselves, "To what or to whom are we opening?" We should never surrender our power to anything but Spirit. If we surrender to a person, an idea, or an institution, we're liable to end up feeling disillusioned and betrayed. Leaders may mislead us, sometimes with the best intentions. After all, even the wisest leader is merely human and may give you bad advice. Groups can be programmed with false information. Every ideology is limited and every institution is flawed and subject to corruption.

If we weren't starved for community ritual and the ecstasy it can engender, we wouldn't be vulnerable to cult seduction. We need to feel that we belong and we need to immerse ourselves in the ec-static, expansive energy of group mind. The more opportunities we have to participate in respectful and empowering spiritual ritual, the less likely that we will succumb to the lure of demagogues or fake gurus.

There is only one way to overcome our fear of group energy and our lack of experience in working with ritual: by gathering with people who have integrity, positive intention, and a commitment to wholeness. Together, we can learn how to open to others without denying our individuality. We can learn how to balance the need for harmony and stability with the need for conflict and change. We can learn how best to use the immense, pulsating energy of a synchro-nized group and how to stand up for our personal truth in the face of dissent or disapproval.

Ever since Western culture discovered the value of individual consciousness, it has worshipped at the altar of individualism. Yet we miss what we have lost. We miss the rapture of ecstatic celebration and the rituals that formerly melded groups of separate individuals into cohesive circles. Listen to Sobonfu Some talking about the role of ritual in her native African village, and you get a glimpse of the ec-static states that ritual can help us access: "In the village, everybody is addicted to ritual. There people experience intimacy not just with their partners, but with the rest of the village, at all times, simply be-cause of the repeated involvement with ritual. There's such a high from this that most conversations are about the ritual that just ended, or about the need for the next ritual. Maybe that's why they don't care about television."[2]

The fundamental purposes of group ritual are to summon Spirit and to heal ourselves and our communities by elevating our group consciousness to a higher level of harmony. We who have traded in ritual for television miss those expanded states of being that liberate us from the wearisome burden of our personalities. Much as we trea-sure the gifts of individuality, we still crave immersion in group energy. Millions of Americans regularly gather for ball games, not simply to witness the game itself—which they could do far more comfortably at home in front of their televisions—but to immerse themselves in the heightened energy field of a large group.

Rhythm

When two people harmonize with each other, love blossoms between them. When an entire group does the same, the result is ecstasy. The easiest and most natural way for a group to harmonize is by dancing, drumming, toning, or chanting. A group is like a harp with many strings. These strings have to be tuned if they are to make beautiful music together. This process of vibrational atunement and rhythmic entrainment does not undo our individual uniqueness; on the contrary, the process supports and enhances it.

Often, people come to my circles harried and worried, frantic and irritable. Usually, the first thing I do is to play music—taped or, even better, live. There's nothing like live music, and especially live drumming, to move the body and heal the soul. The inner chatter dies down when we hear the voice of the great drums. Immersing ourselves in rhythm is like taking a bath in a fresh, cool spring. As we move our bodies in natural, repetitive patterns, our scattered energies begin to return home.

Rhythm is divine law made audible. It's the foundation of our being—the ground we stand upon, the air we breathe, the basic food that sustains our life. As such, it is possibly the most powerful ecstatic tool at our disposal. When we immerse ourselves in rhythm, we dissolve into a pulsating power greater than our individual selves, greater even than our cultural selves. Rhythm demands an attunement of our entire being to time and space so precise and so absolute that in the process, we pass through into other dimensions. Meditation on rhythm is meditation on the relationship of sound to silence. In the duality of sound and silence are contained earth and sky, male and female, life and death, and all the myriad dualities of embodied existence.

In Berkeley, I used to walk by a school yard. Most afternoons, a group of kids, each equipped with a drum, would be gathered around their teacher. At first, it sounded pretty chaotic—you felt like arming yourself with earplugs as you approached. But as the weeks went by, the straggly bunch of kids transformed into a real team. I could tell they were learning a lot more than drumming. They were learning to listen to each other, instead of only to themselves. They were learning about harmony, about group spirit, and about the humbling yet exhilarating ways of nature.

Ecstatic Dance

Right in the middle of a shopping mall, I witnessed an ecstatic dance. The dancer was a little boy, 2 years old at most, a tiny thing in red overalls and bare feet. The joy inside of him was so great that he just couldn't contain it, but had to hop up and down, throwing his chubby arms into the air. His ecstasy was contagious; all around him, people started gathering and laughing, not at him, but with him, and their attention heightened his joy even further. He whooped and crooned, swooped and spun. He hadn't quite mastered balance and coordination, so every now and then he would fall on his butt. Once, his face puckered into a little frown, as if puzzled to find that his body couldn't quite keep up with his spirit. The cloud passed quickly, however. Undaunted, he got up and continued, his face shining with delight.

Dance is both a natural expression of ecstasy and a way of heightening and intensifying it. As children, we all knew how to dance in ecstasy, and we still do—we just need permission and encouragement to reclaim that knowledge.

Dancing is an important element of my circles, and I often see people dancing their way into rapture. No matter how awkward or self-conscious they feel initially, their movements gradually become fluid, soft, and serpentine as ecstasy descends. Sensuously, voluptuously, the awakened serpent begins to undulate through their limbs. "I've never moved like that before," they say afterward, eyes wide with astonishment.

The ecstasy of dance is heightened when it reflects not just our own joy, but the joy of shared spiritual communion. Before the Christian era, all religious traditions worshipped through music and dance. The early Christians, too, danced to celebrate God. In the Middle Ages, however, Christianity condemned dancing as satanic and forbade it in church. The banishment of dance from church has been one of our great cultural tragedies. How can the soul feel welcomed where the body is not allowed to express its joy?

Several years ago, I had the privilege of visiting a Catholic convent in Northern California run by nuns who had made ecstatic dancing a regular part of their service. At the end of the service, a carefully selected piece of music would be played, and all the nuns would leap up from their seats, toss off their black habits to reveal the ordinary clothes they wore underneath, and begin to dance joyfully. It was a moving and heartwarming sight to see these deeply religious women dancing their prayers. A year later, I found out that the pope had intervened. The former abbess had been replaced by a more conservative one, and the dancing had been discontinued. With this type of attitude, is it any wonder the churches are losing their audience?

When I write about music-making and dancing, you might get the impression that ecstatic community means nothing but partying and having a good time. Having a good time is important, but there are two crucial factors that distinguish ecstatic practice from partying. The first is intention. In ecstatic practice our intention is always to open and expand, to awaken to the holy presence, and to invite Spirit to make itself known to us.

Second, ecstatic practice always uses an alternation of movement and stillness, sound and silence, extroversion and introversion. Music and dancing awaken the inner serpent, but instead of simply discharging that energy, we then turn it inward and use it to connect with our deepest Selves. This aspect of containment is essential to ecstatic practice and sets it apart from other forms of celebration. This requires discipline. We have to know how to rein in the galloping horses of body and mind in order to make a 180 degree turn, so that instead of looking outward into the world, we now gaze into the depths of our souls.

The Next Generation

On March 13, 2000, *Time* magazine published a feature article on MDMA, a drug popularly known as Ecstasy. Its popularity among young people has skyrocketed in recent years, causing the U.S. Customs Service to create a special "Ecstasy command center." The article claims that "nationwide, customs officers have already seized more Ecstasy this fiscal year (nearly 3.3 million hits) than in all of last year; in 1997, they seized just 400,000 hits. In a 1998 survey, 8 percent of high school seniors said they had tried Ecstasy, up from 5.8 percent the year before."[3]

The reason young people are taking this drug is that, as its name indicates, it can trigger ecstatic experiences. Well-researched and well-documented as the *Time* article was, it completely ignored the most important question: How should we address this hunger for ecstasy?

Adolescents are arguably the population most in touch with their need for ecstatic music, dance, and ritual. Most of them know, in a way many older people don't, that they need family, community, and spiritual communion. They know that life is barren without it, and they know that music, rhythm, and dance create connections between people. They are fascinated by the invisible world, which they sense holds a key to the meaning of their lives. Underneath their ve-

neer of aloof boredom, many retain the innocence, openness, and ad-
venturousness required to enter the spiritual realms.

For the most part, the older generation has ignored the younger
generation's demand for ec-
static ritual—not out of
malice, but out of ignorance
or a sense of helplessness. Of
course, those of us who grew
up in the 1960s and 1970s
have our own memories of

*If we want to support our young
people, we must acknowledge the
sacred hunger that drives them.*

tapping into that orgiastic energy. Since then, however, most of us
have returned to mainstream society and have adapted to an ecstasy-
deprived way of life.

In the absence of support from their elders, young people have
been experimenting with their own forms of ecstatic ritual. Some
have turned to gangs, cults, and drugs, but others have discovered
healthier forms of group communion. Rap music, for instance, which
we mostly associate with violent sexism, also has another, more spiritual side. Some rap musicians sing about the need for tolerance,
compassion, and kindness. Much of this street music has escaped
commercialization while remaining an important and positive influence in the lives of many young people.

Similarly, the raves at which thousands of young men and women
gather to immerse themselves in a frenzy of music, dance, and often
drugs, are more than just a parent's nightmare. The main elements of
a rave—the ingredients that make a rave a rave—are not sex and
drugs, but rhythm and dance. The younger generation knows that
the pounding beat of the drums can evoke states of trance and can
carry them to mysterious and magical places.

Raves have a long lineage—all ancient cultures had orgiastic ceremonies that used rhythm, music, and dancing, often in conjunction
with mind-altering substances. The difference is that in traditional
cultures, these celebrations were acknowledged as religious rituals,

and the knowledge of how to perform the ritual properly and safely was passed down from generation to generation. Today, young people grope their way by trial and error toward the ecstatic ritual experience for which they yearn.

The hunger for ecstasy is an innate and irrepressible part of who we are. The more you try to repress it, the more it will emerge in distorted, unhealthy ways. If young people find no healthy and wholesome ways of sharing ecstasy with their peers, they will devise their own, perhaps unhealthy or dangerous ones.

If we want to support our young people, we must acknowledge the sacred hunger that drives them and honor them as teachers who remind us of our own need for ecstatic communion.

CHAPTER TWELVE

Go See for Yourself

Every instant that the sun is risen,
if I stand in the temple, or on a balcony,
in the hot fields, or in a walled garden,
my own Lord is making love with me.

—Kabir

Throughout this book, I have said that God is ecstasy and that the way to find ecstasy is through communion with life and with Spirit. I have encouraged you to make ecstasy a priority in your life and to practice the disciplines that connect you with your spiritual source.

But is what I say really true? We've all heard so many different stories about God. Some say that God is ecstasy. Some say that God punishes those who don't behave well. Some say that God is fictitious, a product of wishful thinking. Some of these stories may not make sense to us. For example, if God is really love, why do horrendous things happen?

When you hear conflicting rumors about someone, you know that there's only one way to find out the truth. You have to get to know that person yourself so you can form your own opinion. The same is true in your relationship with Spirit. You can't take my word for it. You have to find out what's true for yourself.

The only person who can show you the way to ecstasy is you. No two people are alike, and nobody can know you from the outside the way you know yourself from the inside. When it comes to matters of the soul, you are the ultimate authority.

The Greek word *authos* means self. Authority, therefore, is knowledge of yourself. Unfortunately, we are trained to see others as authorities and to expect them to tell us what to do and how to live. Many people are so convinced they have no wisdom and no insight that they blindly follow the advice of others and never really look inside.

Asking the Right Questions

Earlier, I invited you to enter into a dialogue with the inner voice of Spirit. If there is one thing I can guarantee, it's that if you really stop and listen long enough, you'll hear this voice and it will answer all your important questions. How can I say this with such conviction? Because I have guided thousands of people to look within, many of whom had assured me that there was nothing there. Not once did anyone find Spirit completely unresponsive.

The real problem lies not in getting answers to our questions, but in asking the right questions. Let me give an example. Let's say that your cat is dying. You love your cat and desperately want her to live, so you turn to Spirit and ask, "How can I heal my cat?"

Chances are that you'll draw a blank. At the most, you'll get some ideas on things you can do to lessen your cat's suffering. The reason is that you are trying to manipulate Spirit by assuming that your cat is destined to live. Your question leaves no space for Spirit to tell you that it is your cat's time to die. You're not willing to hear that. Asking how to heal a cat sounds like a harmless request, but we do not have dominion over the lives of others. We do, on the other hand, have the power to control ourselves. When we ask questions about our own thoughts and actions, we can expect to receive guidance.

Whenever we put limitations on what truths we're willing to hear, we block the channel of communication between ourselves and Spirit. Therefore, the best questions are those that invite guidance without putting conditions on the response. We might ask Spirit, "How can I best support my cat at this time? Is there anything I can do to help her? What should my attitude be?"

Here are some questions that can help you find your own way to ecstasy. They are questions you can ask again and again. Every time you ask, you'll get slightly different answers. Spirit tailors its answers to the person who asks, and that person changes, day by day. Try out these questions and use them to help you find your own.

What is it that I long for?

How can I connect with you now?

How can I stay connected with you throughout the day?

What will it take for me to be happy, right now?

What are my deepest desires?

What can I do today to honor my deepest desires?

What do you want of me?

What is my purpose in life at this time?

What is the most important work I have to do now?

What are the disciplines that support my joy at this time?

Please tell me who I am.

(Describe a difficult situation you are facing.) How can I meet this challenge?

(Describe a recurrent situation that causes you to lose your balance.) How can I stay connected to you throughout this situation?

How can I feel your love for me?

How can I express my love for you?

Why We're Afraid to Look

We need to listen to the voice of Spirit, and we need to look for Spirit in the world around us and in the realms of experience within. The only way to deal with our fears about the nature of God is to see for ourselves. But we're scared, very scared, for three reasons.

ᗺ We're terrified that we'll find out that God isn't there.
ᗺ We're terrified that we'll find out that God doesn't like or approve of us.
ᗺ We're terrified that we'll find out that we don't really like or approve of God.

In other words, we're afraid that our relationship with God isn't going to be the love affairs of our dreams. We feel like someone on a blind date who doesn't yet know whether our date will even show up, let alone whether he or she will be a good match for us.

Except that in this case, there's a lot more at stake. If you decide you and God aren't a good match, what are you going to do about it? Find a different God? In the words of the Islamic prayer, there is no God but God. Or, as the Jewish Shema expresses it, the Lord our God is one.

So it is no wonder that we have a hard time really looking at God. But what, you may ask, am I looking at? And how do I look?

On the opposite page, there's a brief meditation on looking at God. I suggest that you read it to yourself slowly. Then, close your eyes and let the words take you where they will.

Looking at Your Life

God is fully present within every detail of your life. Therefore, another way of looking at God is to look at the truth—*your* truth, which is unlike anyone else's truth, just as your relationship with Spirit will be unlike anyone else's. You simply observe and ac-

TRY THIS...

Look at God.

"I don't know how," says the mind.

Your soul knows how.

Say the words *love, ecstasy, peace, compassion.* Notice what happens in your body. Notice what happens in your emotions. And now and then, notice what happens in your thoughts.

But stay with your body. Put the body first. Put the truth first. Put reality first. That way, your feet stand on firm ground.

Every time your thoughts make you tense, breathe deeply. Relax your body. Let go. This is the practice of dying. It's the sweetest, most compassionate practice.

Let go of shame. Let go of the thought, "I'm unworthy of God's love, of the vision of God, of making love with God." It's a lie.

God has been waiting for you since the beginning of time. God's heart is aching for your love. God's body is aching for your embrace. You are God's lost half. Without you, God will never be whole.

Open your arms to this love. Let go of fear. Ecstasy is perfectly safe when you find it in God's arms. It's nothing less than the joy of coming home to yourself.

Welcome home.

knowledge what you see—the hope, the fear, the disappointment, the joy, the wonder—the whole crazy tangle that is your life.

The ecstatic ground of reality is an open secret; it is there for those who really look—but most of us don't. When you find the time and the courage to step back and simply look at your life, something will begin to happen. At first, it may not feel good. Perhaps you'll feel a sense of waste or regret. You might be painfully aware of missed opportunities or of decisions that caused you a great deal of suffering. But if you keep looking, you can't help but begin to feel a deep sense of wonder. It's as if you realized that you have been looking all along at a great painting, but you've been so close to it that you never realized what it was. All you saw were ugly dark blotches. Then, as you gain a little more distance, you see that the dark blotches are actually just a tiny part of a much larger composition. Out of context, they look ugly, but when you see them next to the greens and blues that surround them, your whole perception changes.

The more you look at your life, the more you begin to appreciate what a work of art it is. You begin to forgive yourself for your mistakes and to forgive life for the ways it has mistreated you. All this happens, not because you will it to happen, but because this is simply how the process of looking works. Slowly, ever so slowly, you fall in love.

People who have found the love of their lives have often said to me, "He is nothing like what I expected," or "I had to let go of all my preconceptions before I could accept that she truly was the one for me."

The same is true of our love affair with life. Life is too big for us. Can this truly be our beloved—this unwieldy, awkward, insane mess? Yes, it can. And the beauty of it is that this lover will never cease to surprise and amaze us. There is no end to the process of mutual discovery, no end to the depth of intimacy that can unfold between yourself and Spirit, no limit to the ecstasy that lies in store for you. But don't take my word for it. Go see for yourself.

Notes

INTRODUCTION
Ecstasy in Daily Life

1. Tukaram, *Says Tuka: Selected Poetry of Tukaram*, trans. Dilip Chitre (New Delhi: Penguin Books India, 1991), 172.
2. Pat Rodegast and Judith Stanton, comp., *Emmanuel's Book: A Manual for Living Comfortably in the Cosmos* (New York: Bantam Books, 1987), 119.

CHAPTER ONE
Meeting God the Lover

1. Jack Kornfield, *A Path with Heart: A Guide through the Perils and Promise of Spiritual Life* (New York: Bantam Books, 1993), 15.
2. Thich Nhat Hanh, *Teachings on Love* (Berkeley, Calif.: Parallax Press, 1997), 63.
3. Thomas Moore, *Meditations: On the Monk Who Dwells in Daily Life* (New York: HarperCollins, 1994), 89.
4. Mechthild von Magdeburg, *Das fliessende Licht der Gottheit* (Stuttgart-Bad Cannstatt: Frommann-Holzboog, 1995), 23. Author's translation.
5. Jalal ad-Din Rumi, *The Essential Rumi*, trans. Coleman Barks with John Moyne (San Francisco: HarperSanFrancisco, 1995), 102–3.
6. Ibid., 37.
7. Jalal ad-Din Rumi, *Open Secret: Versions of Rumi*, trans. John Moyne and Coleman Barks (Putney, Vt.: Threshold Books, 1984), verse 1794.
8. Von Magdeburg, *Das fliessende Licht der Gottheit*, 23. Author's translation.
9. Tukaram, *Says Tuka: Selected Poetry of Tukaram*, trans. Dilip Chitre (New Delhi: Penguin Books India, 1991), 100.
10. Ibid., 193.
11. Knud Rasmussen, *Across Arctic America: Narrative of the Fifth Thule Expedition* (New York: G. P. Putnam's Sons, 1927), 34.

12. A. H. Almaas, *Diamond Heart, Book Two: The Freedom to Be* (Berkeley, Calif.: Diamond Books, 1982), 191.

CHAPTER TWO
The Dance of the Great Hunger

1. Robert Bly, *News of the Universe: Poems of Twofold Consciousness* (San Francisco: Sierra Club Books, 1995), 277.
2. Poem no. 43, in *The Devotional Poems of Mirabai*, trans. A. J. Alston (Delhi: Motilal Banarsidass, 1980), 52.
3. Laurens van der Post, *A Mantis Carol* (London: Hogarth Press, 1975), 114.
4. Ibid.
5. Pema Chödrön, *Start Where You Are: A Guide to Compassionate Living* (Boston: Shambhala, 1994), 100.
6. Ibid., 96.
7. Brian Swimme, *The Universe Is a Green Dragon: A Cosmic Creation Story* (Santa Fe: Bear & Company, 1984), 148.
8. "Our Journey toward Erotic Love: An Interview with Sam Keen, Ph.D.," in Georg Feuerstein, ed., *Enlightened Sexuality: Essays on Body-Positive Spirituality* (Freedom, Calif.: The Crossing Press, 1989), 33.
9. Mother Meera, *Answers* (Ithaca, N.Y.: Meeramma Publications, 1991), 71.
10. Here and throughout, I use the New Jerusalem Bible.
11. Mother Meera, *Answers*, 71.
12. Lance Rancier, *The Sex Chronicles* (Santa Monica, Calif.: General Publishing Group, 1997), 57.
13. Ray Berra, ed., *The Spiritual Athlete: A Primer for the Inner Life* (Olema, Calif.: Joshua Press, 1992), 221.
14. Wes "Scoop" Nisker, *Crazy Wisdom* (Berkeley, Calif.: Ten Speed Press, 1990), 27.

CHAPTER THREE
Banishing the Demon of Shame

1. Author's translation.
2. Sobonfu E. Some, *The Spirit of Intimacy: Ancient Teachings in the Ways of Relationships* (Berkeley, Calif.: Berkeley Hills Books, 1997), 27.
3. St. Augustine, quoted in Elaine Pagels, *Adam, Eve, and the Serpent* (New York: Vintage Books, 1989), 111.
4. Marjorie Shostak, *Nisa: The Life and Words of a !Kung Woman* (New York: Vintage Books, 1983), 269–70.
5. J. Krishnamurti, *Think on These Things*, ed. D. Rajagopal (New York: Harper & Row, 1964), 191.

6. Deepak Chopra, *The Path to Love: Spiritual Strategies for Healing* (New York: Three Rivers Press, 1993), 23.
7. Coleman Barks, trans., *Naked Song/Lalla* (Athens, Ga.: Maypop Books, 1992), 17.
8. Thomas Moore, "Choosing Life: On the Road with 'The Soul of Sex,'" *Spirituality and Health* (winter 1999): 5.
9. Alan Watts, *Nature, Man and Woman* (New York: Pantheon, 1958), 189.

CHAPTER FOUR
Longing for Paradise

1. Maya Deren, *Divine Horsemen: The Living Gods of Haiti* (Kingston, N.Y.: Documentext / McPherson & Co., 1953), 142–45.
2. Jalal ad-Din Rumi, *The Essential Rumi*, trans. Coleman Barks with John Moyne (San Francisco: HarperSanFrancisco, 1995), 272.
3. Deren, *Divine Horsemen*, 145.
4. Holger Kalweit, *Dreamtime and Inner Space* (Boston: Shambhala, 1988), 145.

CHAPTER SIX
The Ecstatic's Discipline

1. Harold Kushner, "To Love and Be Loved," in *Handbook for the Heart*, ed. Richard Carlson and Benjamin Schield (Boston: Little, Brown, 1996), 35.
2. Hongzhi, *Cultivating the Empty Field: The Silent Illumination of Zen Master Hongzhi*, trans. Taigen Daniel Leighton with Yi Wu (San Francisco: North Point Press, 1991), 8–9.
3. Sogyal Rinpoche, *The Tibetan Book of Living and Dying* (San Francisco: HarperSanFrancisco, 1992), 33.
4. Pema Chödrön, *Start Where You Are: A Guide to Compassionate Living* (Boston: Shambhala 1994), 95.
5. Stephen Levine, *A Year to Live: How to Live This Year as If It Were Your Last* (New York: Bell Tower, 1997), 9.
6. Joan Borysenko, "Honoring the Wisdom of Death," *Noetic Sciences Review* no. 32 (winter 1994): 38.

CHAPTER SEVEN
The Practice of Presence

1. *The Gospel of Sri Ramakrishna*, trans. Swami Nikhilananda (New York: Ramakrishna-Vivekananda Center, 1952), 15.
2. William James, *The Varieties of Religious Experience* (London: Longmans, Green, 1935), 399.

3. *The Kabir Book,* by Robert Bly (Boston: Beacon Press, 1977), 24.
4. Pat Rodegast and Judith Stanton, comps., *Emmanuel's Book: A Manual for Living Comfortably in the Cosmos* (New York: Bantam Books, 1985), 121.
5. Frederic and Mary Ann Brussat, *Spiritual Literacy: Reading the Sacred in Everyday Life* (New York: Scribner, 1996), 313.
6. Interview with the author, August 13, 1998.
7. Jalal ad-Din Rumi, *The Essential Rumi,* trans. Coleman Barks with John Moyne (San Francisco: HarperSanFrancisco, 1995), 277.
8. David Steindl-Rast, "Praying the Great Dance," in *The Best of Spiritual Writing 1998,* ed. Philip Zaleski (San Francisco: HarperSanFrancisco, 1999), 264–65.
9. Stephen Mitchell, ed., *The Enlightened Heart: An Anthology of Sacred Poetry* (New York: Harper and Row, 1989), 49.

CHAPTER EIGHT

Beauty

1. Dhyani Ywahoo, *Voices of Our Ancestors: Cherokee Teachings from the Wisdom Fire* (Boston: Shambhala, 1987), 34.
2. David Guterson, *Snow Falling on Cedars* (New York: Vintage Books, 1995), 92.
3. *The Freud/Jung Letters,* ed. William McGuire, trans. Ralph Manheim and R. F. C. Hull, Bollingen series XCIV (Princeton, N.J.: Princeton University Press, 1974), 294.
4. From the *Shivastotra,* quoted in Mark S. G. Dyczkowski, *The Doctrine of Vibration: An Analysis of the Doctrines and Practices of Kashmir Shaivism* (Albany: State University of New York Press, 1987), 150.
5. Thomas Moore, *Care of the Soul: A Guide for Cultivating Depth and Sacredness in Everyday Life* (New York: HarperCollins, 1992), 277–78.
6. Ginette Paris, *Pagan Meditations: The Worlds of Aphrodite, Hestia, and Artemis* (Dallas, Tex.: Spring Publications, 1986), 32.
7. Irma Zaleski, "The Door to Joy," *Parabola: Myth, Tradition, and the Search for Meaning* 23, no. 2 (May 1998): 50.
8. Jalal ad-Din Rumi, *The Essential Rumi,* trans. Coleman Barks with John Moyne (San Francisco: HarperSanFrancisco, 1995), 20.
9. Anne Lamott, *Traveling Mercies: Some Thoughts on Faith* (New York: Pantheon Books, 1999), 65.

CHAPTER NINE

Sexual Ecstasy

1. Pat Rodegast and Judith Stanton, comps., *Emmanuel's Book: A Manual for Living Comfortably in the Cosmos* (New York: Bantam Books, 1985), 204.

2. Sobonfu E. Some, *The Spirit of Intimacy: Ancient Teachings in the Ways of Relationships* (Berkeley, Calif.: Berkeley Hills Books, 1997), 41.

CHAPTER TEN
The Sacred Marriage

1. Frederic and Mary Ann Brussat, *Spiritual Literacy: Reading the Sacred in Everyday Life* (New York: Scribner, 1996), 417.
2. Sam Keen, *Fire in the Belly* (New York: Bantam Books, 1992), 12.
3. Stephen Kiesling, "If You Think Your Marriage Is Divine, It Likely Is," *Spirituality Magazine* (winter 1999): 13.
4. Stephen Levine and Ondrea Levine, "The Heart Is Always Open," in *Handbook of the Heart*, ed. Richard Carlson and Benjamin Shield (Boston: Little, Brown, 1996), 17.
5. Sobonfu E. Some, *The Spirit of Intimacy: Ancient Teachings in the Ways of Relationships* (Berkeley, Calif.: Berkeley Hills Books, 1997), 26.
6. *The Upanishads: Breath of the Eternal*, trans. Swami Prabhavananda and Frederick Manchester (Hollywood, Calif.: Vedanta Press, 1947), 142.

CHAPTER ELEVEN
The Power of Community

1. Story retold with the permission of Atum O'Kane.
2. Sobonfu E. Some, *The Spirit of Intimacy: Ancient Teachings in the Ways of Relationships* (Berkeley, Calif.: Berkeley Hills Publishing, 1997), 52–53.
3. John Cloud, "Drugs: Pipelines to Ecstasy," *Time*, March 13, 2000, 64–66.

Credits

Excerpts from poems by Tukaram on pp. 4, 25–26, and 26 are from *Says Tuka: Selected Poetry of Tukaram*, translated by Dilip Chitre, copyright © 1991. Reprinted with the permission of Penguin Books India Pvt. Ltd. and the translator.

Quotations from Kabir on pp. 11, 36, and 140 are from *The Kabir Book* by Robert Bly, copyright © 1971, 1977 by Robert Bly, © 1977 by the Seventies Press. Reprinted with the permission of Beacon Press, Boston.

Excerpts from poems by Rumi on pp. 17, 89, and 164 are from *The Essential Rumi*, translations by Coleman Barks with John Moyne, copyright © 1995. Reprinted with the permission of Threshold Books, Brattleboro, Vermont.

Quotation on p. 37 from Mirabai, "I have felt the swaying of the elephant's shoulders," from *News of the Universe: Poems of Twofold Consciousness* by Robert Bly, copyright © 1980, 1995 by Robert Bly. Reprinted with the permission of Sierra Club Books.

Poem by Lalla on p. 76 from *Naked Song/Lalla*, translations by Coleman Barks, Maypop Books, Athens, Georgia, copyright © 1992 by Coleman Barks. Reprinted with the permission of Coleman Barks.

Excerpts on pp. 86–87 from Maya Deren, *Divine Horsemen: The Living Gods of Haiti*, copyright © 1953. Reproduced with the permission of McPherson and Company, Kingston, New York.

Poem by Dogen on p. 151 from *The Enlightened Heart: An Anthology of Sacred Poetry*, edited by Stephen Mitchell, copyright © 1989. Reprinted with the permission of Harper and Row, New York.

Story on pp. 205–7 about Shlomo Carlebach by Atum O'Kane, retold by the author with the permission of Atum O'Kane.

About the Author

Jalaja (pronounced DJA-la-dja) Bonheim, Ph.D., is a counselor, workshop leader, public speaker, and one of the most engaging teachers of nonreligious spirituality today. Raised and educated in Austria and Germany, she has devoted many years to the study of classical Indian temple dance, mythology, and Hindu and Buddhist meditation. Her previous books include *Aphrodite's Daughters: Women's Sexual Stories* and *The Journey of the Soul and Goddess: A Celebration in Art and Literature*. She is the founder and director of the Institute for Circlework, which provides training and education in the art of spiritually based group leadership.

For information on events and workshops with Jalaja Bonheim, visit her Web site at www.meetingsinsacredspace.com, or write to: Meetings in Sacred Space, P.O. Box 847, Ithaca, NY 14851. Although she welcomes correspondence from readers, she regrets that she is not able to respond to every letter.